Praise for *The Gift of Shyness*

"In *The Gift of Shyness*, Dr. Alexander offers real-world solutions for shy people who are sincerely interested in finding their soul mate. *The Gift of Shyness* works!"—Dr. Patricia Allen, KRLA radio host and best-selling author of *Getting to "I Do"*

"*The Gift of Shyness* is an absolute must-read for shy men and women who want to shed their wallflower image forever!"—Don Gabor, best-selling author of *How to Start a Conversation and Make Friends*

"Entertaining and practical. It shows the reader how to use shyness as a way to engage in a meaningful relationship."—Migene González-Wippler, author of *Santeria* and *What Happens After Death*

"This book is a must-have for anyone who is serious about relationships."—Myreah Moore, America's Dating Coach and author of *Date Like a Man*

"*The Gift of Shyness* is a gift to the millions of shy people who are so often overlooked by the 'relationship experts.' Embracing your shyness is exactly what's needed to counter the common (and absurd) advice to 'get over it.' "—Gregory J. P. Godek, author of *1001 Ways to Be Romantic*

"What an incredible book Dr. Alexander Avila has written! This book is a blessing for shy people around the world because it shows shy people how to use their gifts of shyness to bring lasting love and romance in their lives."—Michael Webb, author of *The RoMANtic's Guide*

EMBRACE YOUR SHY SIDE AND FIND
YOUR SOUL MATE

THE Gift OF
SHYNESS

DR. ALEXANDER AVILA

A FIRESIDE BOOK
Published by Simon & Schuster
NEW YORK • LONDON • TORONTO • SYDNEY • SINGAPORE

FIRESIDE
Rockefeller Center
1230 Avenue of the Americas
New York, NY 10020

FIRESIDE and colophon are registered trademarks
of Simon & Schuster, Inc.

The Gift of Shyness® is a registered trademark of Alexander Avila.
ImprovTherapy® is a registered trademark of Alexander Avila.

Designed by Elina Nudelman

Manufactured in the United States of America

3 5 7 9 10 8 6 4 2

Library of Congress Cataloging-in-Publication Data

Avila, Alexander.
The gift of shyness : embrace your shy side and find your soul mate /
Alexander Avila.
p.   cm.
Includes bibliographical references and index.
1. Bashfulness. 2. Introversion. 3. Love. 4. Man-woman
relationships. I. Title.
BF575.B3 A94 2002
155.2'32—dc21   2001040508

ISBN 0-7432-0075-6

To Shy and Introvert People Everywhere:

*You are my brothers and sisters, and together
we will revolutionize the social world.*

Acknowledgments

To my friends and family: Without your love and support, I would not have been able to accomplish this grand venture. Thank you from the bottom of my heart. That's you, Andy.

To Marcela Landres, my supremely talented editor at Simon & Schuster: Thank you for your wise guidance and counsel in helping to make this book what it is.

To Sheree Bykofsky, my incredible, warm, and loving agent, who is a marvelous person in every sense of the word. Thanks for all your love and support.

Contents

Why Shyness Is a Wonderful Romantic Gift

The Truth About Being Single and Shy

Desperate for answers, Janet made up her mind to call the local radio psychologist for advice about her shyness. As a thirty-three-year-old graphic designer and business owner, Janet was successful in every aspect of her life, except romance. In fifteen years of dating she had experienced numerous short-lived romantic encounters, almost all of which could easily be called failures. Her problem was always the same: She was too shy to approach the men she was really interested in, and too shy to say no to the men she didn't want. Oh, how badly she wanted a solution.

"Hello, caller. What's your name and problem?"

"Um, my name is Janet, and my problem is I'm shy with men."

"How long have you been shy with men?"

"Fifteen years."

"Fifteen years. Come on, Janet. You can stop being shy if you want to. Tell me one good reason why you're still shy. Tell me."

"I don't know, I'm not sure."

"Yes, you do. Think of one reason why you're still shy."

Silence.

"Come on, Janet, we don't have all day here. Tell me.

"Hello, Janet. Hello? Hello?"

Shyness is a loaded word. For many people it conjures up images of a hopeless nerd who can't string two words together without stuttering or blushing, a lonesome wallflower who is destined to be alone for the rest of his or her life.

Let's face it: To be shy in our society is to be considered less than a complete human being. Shyness has been defined as a harmful psychological state that causes people to withdraw from others because they're extremely fearful of being judged or criticized. Shy people have been labeled anxious, withdrawn, even antisocial. If you're shy, experts tell you to banish shyness, overcome it, kick it out of your life. They advise you to talk more, take more social risks, go out more—even if you don't feel like it.

Want more so-called advice? How about making a schedule of places to go, smiling, making eye contact, flirting? Why don't you become a real person, for God's sake? Stop being such a shy basket case. Speak up. What's the matter with you? Do you want to spend the rest of your life alone, with the remote control as your only companion?

There's only one tiny problem with the advice of these so-called shyness experts: They are wrong—dead wrong. These pundits (most of whom are not shy and have never been shy) don't know anything about the real you. In fact, they are not aware of a truth so profound that its simplicity may shock you:

SHYNESS IS ACTUALLY A GIFT OF GENTLENESS, SENSITIVITY, AND SELF-REFLECTION, AND YOU, AS A SHY PERSON—JUST THE WAY YOU ARE RIGHT NOW—ARE ONE OF THE MOST DESIRABLE PEOPLE ON EARTH.

That's right. By virtue of owning the Gift of Shyness, you are a very attractive human being. As part of your shy personality package, you possess wonderful romantic qualities, such as conscientiousness, soft-spokenness, sensitivity, loyalty, and compassion. You are the type of person who is fervently desired by intelligent, attractive, and sincere individuals everywhere, many of whom would be captivated by your sweet, kind presence if they had the opportunity to get to know you better.

Yes, shyness is the perfect romantic gift for those who know how to unwrap its delicate package. Unfortunately, there are so many inaccuracies—so much misleading information—about shyness, dating, and love that shy people are often confused about the best way to approach their romantic lives.

The obstacle that prevents you from entering a relationship with the love of your life has nothing to do with your shyness. Rather, your dating struggles are created by the battle between two opposing sides of your personality: the Self-Observer and the Actor.

The Self-Observer, or simply the *Observer*, is the self-conscious, reflective part of your mind. It's the mental mirror that is always observing you and constantly evaluating your social performance through the eyes of other people. The Observer is constantly asking: Am I coming across OK? Do other people like me? Am I making a social blunder?

At the other end of the spectrum lies the *Actor*: the playful and free-flowing part of your mind. The Actor is the side of you that acts spontaneously in social situations without worrying too much about what others think. It's the fun-loving part of your mind that is perfectly happy being in the moment.

Think of your personality as a battleground, with two opposing camps: the Actor and the Observer. Some people ally themselves more with the Actor, some with the Observer. Others choose neutral ground and prefer to be friends with both. Shy people are usually too closely allied with their Observers; they have too much of the self-critical Observer—and not enough of the spontaneous Actor—in their personalities. As a result, they become excessively self-conscious and worried about making mistakes and looking foolish in social settings. These Observer-dominated shy people often freeze in social interactions—so afraid to look silly or incompetent that they're unable to say or do anything at all.

At the other extreme are the people who have too much of the Actor. These selfish and inconsiderate individuals rarely think about the consequences of their actions. Although the Actor can contribute greatly to the development of social confidence and spontaneity, people who are 100 percent Actor-driven tend to go overboard and act in childish ways—giving in to their immature impulses and focusing on their own needs without considering the impact of their reckless behavior on others.

Socially successful people, by contrast, occupy the middle ground and are on friendly terms with both their Actors and their Observers. They have what is known as the Actor-Observer Balance—the ideal mixture of spontaneous Actor and self-reflective Observer. They have just enough Actor to make sure they act naturally and spontaneously in social situations, and just the right amount of Observer to help them correct their social mistakes and improve their romantic results.

Throughout this book you will learn field-proven techniques, strategies, and exercises to help you develop the ideal blend of Actor and Observer so you can establish a successful presence in the social world and achieve romantic success. Before you create this ideal combination, however, you need to realize just how much your overactive Observer has controlled you until now, and how much it has prevented you from finding love. When the Observer controls your personality, you are incapable of acting freely and intelligently. You become too self-critical and self-conscious, too quick to chastise yourself for not being clever enough, attractive enough, or good enough to attract and hold the affections of the person you desire.

If you suffer from an overly domineering Observer who keeps you mired in the dust of self-loathing, realize this: There are a lot of us out there just like you. In fact, I too have been in your shoes. Unlike most shyness researchers and authors, I know firsthand what it's like to be shy and tormented by an unrelenting Observer.

I still remember my shy high school days and how desperate I was to go out with one of the prettiest girls I'd ever seen, Cathy. Beautiful, with flowing blond hair, she was also the top female student in my school, was skilled in several sports, and had a terrific personality. Although I felt I was equally talented, I told myself I was too shy and unattractive to be successful with her. Why even try when I was sure she would reject me?

Despite my feelings of inadequacy, I felt driven to connect with her; I just had to. Finally, I gathered up all my courage to ask her to a school dance. Too embarrassed to call from home, I walked half a mile to a public phone booth and called her. Shaking like mad, I panicked when she answered, and, in embarrassment, I hung up.

Again, breathing heavily and desperately, I dialed her number and heard her sweet hello—but again the thought of talking to her and facing rejection was too painful, and I hung up. On the third try, she spoke before I could hang up once more: "You're disgusting. Don't ever call here again!" Those were the last words I heard from her. After that night I never talked to her again, and I felt rejected, humiliated, and lost.

Although it was very painful at the time, I realize now that my shyness was not to blame for my decision to hang up on Cathy. The villain was my unrelenting Observer, the cracked mental mirror through which I saw myself, the broken glass that branded me a "dating loser" who had no business being with an incredible and beautiful person like Cathy. By believing in this faulty mirror's image, I set myself up for failure. Because I expected her to reject me, I acted in a self-defeating way that brought about the very result I was fearing.

Today, even though I hold a doctorate in clinical psychology and am well versed in shyness research and literature, I still have that shy boy inside me. The only difference is that now, rather than hovering over him like a condemning critic, I allow him to act freely and spontaneously as he fully expresses his shy, gentle traits. Now I lovingly embrace this shy creature as a caring soul full of desirable romantic qualities ready to spring forth in the right context and for the right person. Although I now understand how valuable I am as a shy person, it took me years to get to this point. In the meantime I criticized myself mercilessly for my perceived social flaws, and I felt doomed to a loveless existence.

How about you? How many times have you tormented yourself because you weren't as witty, talkative, or expressive as you should have been? How many times have you second-guessed yourself for the things you should have said (or shouldn't have said) when dealing with a potential romantic partner? How many times have you felt anxiety, perhaps outright terror, when you were near someone you were very attracted to? Chances are you've experienced these thoughts and feelings many times as a shy person.

Yet no matter how many times you have attacked yourself for being shy and socially inadequate in the past, things are about to change. In the pages to come you will learn a groundbreaking approach for achieving the Actor-Observer Balance—that state of mind in which you have just enough Actor to keep you acting spontaneously, without self-consciousness, and just enough Observer to give you intelligent feedback on how others are reacting to you.

This new approach—ImprovTherapy—combines the most powerful techniques of psychodrama (a therapeutic method that utilizes role playing) and improvisational acting (theater games designed to improve acting skills and spontaneity) to help you become a spontaneous, self-accepting, and free-flowing person who is, at the same time, intelligent, aware, and conscientious.

As a shyness researcher for the past seven years, I have helped more than one thousand shy individuals use ImprovTherapy to develop a healthy Actor-Observer Balance—en route to enjoying happy and successful romantic lives. You can do it too. With the Gift of Shyness as your romantic guide, you will transform your shyness into a true dating advantage on your way to finding your soul mate. In Chapter 4 you will take the Shy Type Quiz and learn the secrets of your unique social style. Then, in the rest of the book, you will learn the truth about shyness, dating, and romance from your perspective—the shy person's viewpoint. You will learn, among other things, the answers to the following important questions:

- What is the real definition of shyness?
- Why are shy men and women in the twenty-first century at greater risk of experiencing romantic loneliness than at any other time in history?
- How can I achieve the Actor-Observer Balance?
- How can I develop the utmost romantic self-confidence so I can navigate the social world without fear or self-doubt?
- How can I tap into my natural gifts as a shy person to go out on more enjoyable dates and eventually meet my ideal romantic partner?
- How can I experience a satisfying and rewarding sex life as a shy person?
- How can I use my shy-sensitive nature to develop and maintain a lasting relationship with my ideal mate?

CHAPTER 2

It's a Shy World After All

Beverly had a secret.

At her personal injury law firm, thirty-two-year-old Beverly was one of the hardest working and feistiest paralegals anyone had ever seen. Only five foot one, but packing a lot of personality for her size, Beverly impressed friends and foes alike with her plucky attitude and flair for the legal game.

What her co-workers didn't know was that Beverly was a closet shy person: someone who was very skilled at covering up her shyness at work but who fell apart in social encounters. Whenever she was face-to-face with an attractive man, a paralyzing wave of anxiety would sweep over Beverly, making her incapable of stringing two sentences together without blushing like a schoolgirl.

For years Beverly had lived a double life—confident and talkative at work, shy and fearful in her dating life. She often wondered if there were others like her, shadow shy people who lurked on the fringes of the social world, never quite sure where they fit, nervously counting the minutes until Monday morning, when they could slip into their safe and comfortable work roles.

Now it was 6:30 on a Friday evening and time to go home. No longer able to hide under her work persona, Beverly had to be herself: a shy single woman in the big bad dating world. It wasn't a very pleasant place to be.

How common is shyness? At least 40 percent of Americans—more than 100 million people—consider themselves shy, and the percentage is as high as 60 percent in countries such as Japan. Millions more may not report themselves as being shy, but when it comes to the prospect of dating someone they're really attracted to, they, too, have a shy side. These individuals may be ultraconfident in work and other aspects of life, but when Mr. or Ms. Right stares them in the face, their hearts flutter and their knees get weak.

You may not realize it, but the person next to you right now may be a very shy person when it comes to dating and romance. Underneath that smiling social mask may lie a secretly shy person who is a pro at keeping his or her shyness hidden, a deep, dark secret only a therapist or priest will ever know. Because these closet shy people are ashamed of their shyness, they will do everything possible to avoid even the slightest suspicion that they are shy. They will fool you with their confident, outgoing, and talkative ways, even though, deep down, they are really very shy.

As you read this, you may be saying to yourself: "I'm just like that—a secretly shy person. Some of my acquaintances and co-workers don't even know I'm shy." And you can just imagine what some of them might think if they knew: You, shy? I don't believe it. You seem so outgoing and confident. I never imagined you could be a social loser like that.

Let's face it: The real reason shy people try to disguise their shyness is that many influential members of society—researchers, psychologists, and psychiatrists—tell them it's bad to be shy. Shy people have been unfairly described as tight-lipped, slow, dumb, shrinking, cowardly, fearful, antisocial, suspicious, and secretive.

Researchers tell shy people they suffer from a personality deficit. Psychologists tell shy people their shyness is what makes them feel flawed, weak, and socially inferior. Psychiatrists tell shy people they need to take medication to eliminate their shyness. It's no wonder, then, that shy people everywhere go to great pains to cover up their shyness. To acknowledge being shy is to publicly admit social failure, to feel like pariahs, to announce they are outcasts who don't belong with the rest of normal society.

Many shy people are not appreciated for who they are because Western society promotes a social style that is contrary to the shy person's sensitive and reflective nature. In the media, in schools, and at home, children are told they must be aggressive, outgoing, extraverted, sociable, talkative, and straightforward if they want to be successful and happy.

There's nothing wrong, of course, with being assertive, direct, and outgoing. These are valuable traits that can help you succeed in life. The problem arises when shy people, who may not possess these traits in abundance, are not respected and revered for what they bring to the world: their quiet, sensitive, and inward-focused natures.

Research shows that, rather than praising their shy children for being sensitive, many U.S. mothers tend to feel concerned, disappointed, guilty, and embarrassed when their children turn out to be shy. Consequently, these mothers may unwittingly take their feelings out on their children by blaming them for being shy. This response, in turn, lowers shy children's self-esteem and makes them feel unworthy for being who they really are.

Contrast the Western approach with the view of shy children in China. Quiet children in China are called *guai*, which means "good" or "well-behaved." Children who are sensitive are considered *dong shi* (understanding), favorite Chinese words used to praise a child. Because Chinese mothers have a more accepting attitude toward their children's shyness, Chinese children grow up feeling more comfortable with their shy-sensitive natures.

What Is Shyness Really?

For many years academics and researchers have examined two types, or definitions, of shyness: one based on fear, the other on self-consciousness. Let's look at each of these traditional definitions.

What Am I Afraid Of?

Duane, a forty-two-year-old African American kindergarten teacher, was known as a terrifically nice guy. He would help his fellow teachers any time they needed a favor, and he always had a ready smile and kind word when someone was down. Good looking, with a buff body and cocoa brown skin, Duane seemed like the perfect catch. Many of his colleagues wondered why he had never married.

What they didn't know was that Duane was petrified whenever he was around a woman he found attractive, especially in social settings like nightclubs or dances. To begin with, the lights, crowds, and loud noises at these places made Duane nervous and agitated; he always felt shaky and uncomfortable as soon as he walked in. Things would go from bad to worse when he caught a whiff of a pretty lady he wanted to meet: His mouth would get dry, his heart would pound, and he would get a hot, itchy feeling on his face that would later turn into a nasty rash. Duane would be so miserable that he would never speak to any of the ladies, and he would suffer in silence until he could make his quick escape home.

After years of these social misadventures, Duane finally called it quits on the dating scene. He decided it would be better, not to mention healthier, to stay home with his dog, stamp collection, and PC, than to risk the dangers of the singles scene.

Researchers have described shyness as a form of communication fear—the anxiety that shy people experience when they talk (or think about talking) to others. According to this view, shy people are petrified of being ridiculed, rejected, embarrassed, and humiliated in social settings. To protect themselves from these painful feelings, shy people avoid or try to escape from intimidating social situations. Although they may succeed at getting away, shy people still pay a price, in the form of uncomfortable physical symptoms such as blushing, rapid heart rate, shallow breathing, and excessive perspiration.

If you're shy, you may have experienced these anxiety reactions in intimidating social situations. Although you may have suffered from anxiety in the past, the truth is that anxiety and fear are not the main factors in your shyness. According to research, one of the most important elements of your shyness is something known as emotional reactivity—how sensitive you are, and how much you react emotionally, to the outside world.

As a shy person, you probably react more intensely to the envi-

ronment that non-shy people do. You're more likely to suffer dis-
comfort when you're exposed to bright lights, loud sounds, and
harsh words. Because you have this special sensitivity, you can be
hurt more easily when you think others are likely to criticize or
judge you. To protect your tender emotional shell, you may withdraw before others have a chance to really harm you.

For some shy people this emotional reactivity appears to have
a genetic base. In one classic study infants were exposed to various stimuli, such as brightly colored toys moved back and forth in
front of their faces. Twenty percent of the infants reacted in an extremely anxious manner: vigorously waving their arms, kicking their
legs, arching their backs, and crying. These highly excitable babies—
called high reactives—appeared to have easily arousable nervous
systems, which made them respond intensely to a disruption in their
environment. Another 40 percent of the children were more calm
and did not fret or cry as much in response to the same events. These
calmer children were called low reactives because they didn't react
as intensely.

When the same children were interviewed in early adolescence
(thirteen to fourteen years old), the researchers found that social
phobia (the excessive and persistent fear of being embarrassed in social situations) was more frequent among the high reactives than
among the low reactives. These findings offer substantial evidence
to support the view that a number of shy people are born with delicate nervous systems that cause them to react intensely to the outside world.

Not all shy people, however, are born with this heightened sensitivity. Some develop it later in life, perhaps as the result of a difficult
upbringing or as a response to stressful changes like moving to a new
place and leaving friends behind, or losing a mate to breakup, divorce, or death. As these individuals attempt to cope with challenging circumstances, they may adopt a mind-set that is similar to that
of shy people born with a highly sensitive disposition: They are
deeply affected by other people's moods and emotions and can
react with intense fear and self-doubt if they feel others will reject
or abandon them.

Regardless of how a person develops this strong sensitivity, it's
important to recognize the positive and negative aspects of this spe-

cial personality trait. On the upside, shy people can use their intense emotional natures to love people more deeply and faithfully—their naturally empathetic personalities are tailor-made for profound and lasting relationships. On the downside, shy people may experience more emotional pain because they can be easily hurt by others; they are more sensitive to real or imagined criticism and rejection. In their minds they may already see themselves as rejected or embarrassed, and they can easily manufacture feelings of anxiety, disappointment, and self-doubt.

Although they may feel deeply, shy people don't always show what they're feeling. They can appear placid and almost emotionless at first glance because of their private and self-protective natures. In their minds, however, shy people are capable of entertaining a vivid symphony of colorful emotions. They will let their emotions out only when they feel safe and comfortable, and when they're certain they won't be judged or criticized.

To be happy in life, shy people need to respect their sensitive natures. Rather than criticize themselves for being fearful, thin-skinned, or socially inadequate, they need to stand up for themselves and declare: "I'm a sensitive and loving person, and I deserve a wonderful relationship."

One of the ways shy people can protect their sensitive natures is by avoiding harsh environments and intrusive people. Shy people, unfortunately, often get the opposite advice: Some dating programs, for example, encourage shy people to get out more, and go to parties, nightclubs, or bars to meet people. In reality, these crowded, noisy, and pushy environments are usually the worst places for shy people because they violate their delicate emotional balance and leave them feeling like worn-out rags.

Be smart. Preserve your social and emotional energy for activities you have carefully selected, places where you have a good chance of meeting nice people in a comfortable, relaxed, and low-pressure manner.

Avoid people who don't appreciate your shy-sensitive nature. Always remind yourself of the biblical advice "Don't throw your pearls to the pigs." Think about it: Would you give a pearl to a drunken bum on the street who will sell it for liquor at the first opportunity? Of course not. In the same way, save your pearl of sensitivity for your beloved, someone who will truly respect, cherish, and even worship you for the type of person you are. When you reframe your shyness as social sensitivity instead of frozen fear, you can begin to use your natural social strengths to attract a desirable partner and achieve a happy love life. (Look for tips on how to do this in Part 3.)

While you can use the emotional component of shyness as a romantic asset, there *is* one aspect of shyness that can be more difficult to deal with: the finger-pointing trait known as self-consciousness.

Why Is Everyone Staring at Me?

Eyes, eyes, eyes everywhere. That was one of the strongest images twenty-nine-year-old Susan, a pretty, auburn-haired, divorced beautician, remembered about growing up in a controlling family headed by a critical, abusive father. In her mind Susan would always see her father's eyes following her around the house, staring at her, quick to pounce if she made a mistake.

When she started counseling for her shyness, Susan was obsessed with the idea that everyone was staring at her. She kept having nightmares about big eyes that followed her everywhere, judging her, condemning her, and criticizing her for being socially inadequate. At social events Susan would constantly second-guess herself: No, I shouldn't have said that. I better keep my mouth shut or I'll really make a fool out of myself.

No matter how much she tried to convince herself that it was all in her head, Susan was dead sure everyone in the room was staring at her, ready to ridicule her for making a mistake. Oh, if only she could get rid of those condemning eyes, thought Susan. She could have a normal social life if she could nix those damning eyes.

Another popular definition of shyness focuses on self-consciousness: an excessive preoccupation with the self. Self-consciously shy people are obsessed with the idea that others are looking at them, judging them, criticizing them.

These self-consciously shy people have a strong sense of the Observer—the part of their mind that is constantly scrutinizing them and pointing out their social flaws. The Observer makes you feel like an inferior social creature, relentlessly reminding you of your social inadequacies: "You never say the right thing. You never do the right thing. Don't screw up again, or you'll be alone for life." Shy people are especially skilled at using this harsh spotlight to keep the focus on themselves, magnifying any of their (often imagined) weaknesses while ignoring the real flaws of the people they're spending time with.

Researchers have found that the more men think about women as being attractive, poised, and competent, the more anxious men feel when talking to them. This demonstrates the way shy people constantly evaluate themselves in social settings, wasting much of their valuable time and energy comparing themselves (usually unfavorably) with others. Because their Observers only let them see their own magnified flaws and inadequacies, shy people often feel they can never measure up to the awe-inspiring people they're interested in. As a result, they often feel nervous, inferior, and frustrated when they're face-to-face with someone they're really attracted to. The end result? Shy people withdraw from further social contact and miss out on promising romantic opportunities.

Although self-consciousness as manifested by the Observer can be unhealthy and damaging, there are some positive aspects to the Observer. First, the Observer can give you a realistic source of social feedback. When you use the Observer intelligently, you will be aware of the social mistakes you make, and you will be able to learn from them.

At the same time, the Observer can serve as your conscience and act as the ideal counterbalance to your freewheeling, spontaneous Actor. If your Actor tempts you to do something that is rude, selfish, or inappropriate, the Observer will warn you to slow down and consider the consequences.

Finally, because the Observer makes you so reflective, you're comfortable going inside yourself and pondering the important questions of life. This makes you a deep, interesting person who has a lot to offer a potential mate. You're the type of individual who can keep your partner intrigued with your remarkable intellect and deep insights about the things that really matter in life.

The New Definition of Shyness

The time has come to create a new view of shyness that accentuates the positive and celebrates shy people for their marvelous contributions to the world. Here is the positive, transformative definition of shyness that all shy people can embrace from now on:

**SHYNESS IS A LIFE-ENHANCING STATE
OF EXTRAORDINARY SOCIAL SENSITIVITY AND
PROFOUND SELF-REFLECTION.**

With this shy-centric definition, the burden has shifted from the shy person. The shy individual no longer has to fight social convention or medical opinion to prove he or she is psychologically healthy or socially adequate. This definition assumes that every shy person is gifted with positive social qualities and life-affirming talents.

At the same time this new paradigm recognizes what can happen when people misuse their shyness. If, for example, shy people don't protect their sensitive natures and instead thrust themselves into abusive or socially aggressive environments, they will probably suffer from anxiety, discouragement, and low self-esteem. Their problem is not their shy-sensitive nature but the way they use it to interact with the world. Another possibility: A naturally reflective shy person may go to the extreme of scrutinizing his or her every social move. Now the balance has shifted from a healthy combination of Actor and Observer to an Observer-dominated existence that is painful and unproductive.

Although they face challenges, shy people have powerful tools at their disposal to help them transform their shyness into a lifelong asset. As long as they see shyness as their friend, and not their enemy, they can begin to build the ideal framework to meet their romantic goals.

IF SHYNESS HAS A CAUSE, IS THERE A CURE?

For years researchers have tried to determine a cause for shyness. The theories have ranged from a biological approach (shy people are physiologically and genetically different from non-shy people) to a learning theory (shy people learn how to be shy as a reaction to their environment).

The biological theory suggests that certain areas of the brain known to cause fear reactions are more easily activated in shy or highly reactive individuals. These areas release adrenaline, causing shy individuals to experience intense emotions, particularly fear and anxiety, in reaction to potentially threatening events.

In support of this theory, highly reactive infants have been found to have higher resting heart rates, which can be detected even before birth, while the infant is still in utero. Also, when exposed to stress and unfamiliar people and objects, their pupils dilate sooner, their vocal cords are more tense, and their saliva contains more cortisol, the hormone that's released when people are under stress.

Alternatively, researchers have theorized that a person's early learning experiences can significantly affect the way he or she reacts to the world. For example, consider the case of a nine-year-old boy who is harshly criticized by his father whenever he starts singing and horsing around at home. The father makes the boy feel inferior and self-conscious by calling him a goof-off and scolding him incessantly. The boy has now learned that it's bad to be loud and stand out. As a result, he will seek refuge from his father's criticism by withdrawing into his private inner world. Whenever he finds himself in a social situation in which he feels he may be judged or criticized, he will automatically experience the same anxiety, shame, and self-consciousness that he used to feel with his father. When that happens he will quickly disappear into his shy shell and do everything possible to shield himself from the harsh spotlight of social judgment.

Although the learning theory has its proponents, a good argument can be made that both learning and genetic factors may be involved in the creation of a shy person. Regardless of which view you support, there remains one essential fact: Shyness is not usually a passing phase. For many people shyness is an ingrained aspect of their personalities, an important part of them, just like their hands or eyes.

If shyness is an integral part of a person's psychological, emotional, and physiological makeup, then it seems ludicrous to talk about finding the "cure" for shyness or giving medication to wipe out shyness. That would be like trying to get rid of someone's brown eyes because other people didn't like brown. If you "cured" your shyness, you might also lose many of the positive aspects of your shy nature, including sensitivity and self-reflection. Rather than change your basic shy nature, the best approach is to embrace the beneficial parts of your shyness while transforming those elements that can be problematic.

Who Makes the First Move?

Carmen, a twenty-four-year-old graduate student, was a "rules" girl. She was a follower of the best-selling dating book *The Rules,* which taught that the best man-catching strategy was always to wait for a man to call, to let him take the lead.

The rules would work perfectly in her case, thought Carmen, except for a couple of minor details: She was shy and so was the guy she was interested in, *papi chulo* Pedro, a thirty-two-year-old, bronze-skinned Guatemalan construction worker who even had muscles on his fingertips.

They had played hide-and-seek at their local church group for months now, making wavering eye contact and mumbling a few words at each other. But it wasn't going anywhere; both of them were too shy to make a move. Now Pedro was moving to a new church, and her window of opportunity was slamming shut. Carmen pondered the issue: Should she approach Pedro if she could talk herself into it? Or should she wait for the shy Pedro to play the manly role and ask her out?

She was confused, and time was running out.

In the last thirty years most of the research on shyness and dating has focused on men. Because men have been considered the initiators in dating, it was assumed they suffered the most from being shy. After all, if a man was shy, he wouldn't approach women and he would rarely get any dates. By contrast, if a woman was shy, especially if she was considered physically attractive, she could simply lay back and let the man do all the work; her shyness would not be that big a deal.

Back in 1985 researchers found that shy men tended to describe themselves as anxious whenever they thought they were going to be evaluated in a social situation. They used their anxiety as an excuse or fallback explanation in case they performed poorly in a social situation. Shy women didn't feel this need to cover up any potentially poor performance by claiming anxiety. The researchers explained this result by pointing out how shy women, when faced with anxiety-provoking social situations, find it easy to fall back into traditionally passive female roles (smiling, nodding, playing coy and hard to get), while letting the men take the more active role.

Only six years later, however, another study found that women were taking a more assertive role in dating: 54 percent of the women in the study reported initiating one or more dates with men within the last month, and 72 percent reported initiating one or more dates within the last six months. The researchers concluded that women were no longer willing to wait and hope that men would take the lead in initiating a date.

Although in some parts of the world men may still appear to initiate a lot of the dating interaction, women are beginning to bear more of the romantic burden. As gender equality becomes more of a reality, women are increasingly taking the early dating initiative. Even teenage girls are doing a lot of the calling as teenage boys wait at home for the phone to ring.

Moreover, in places where men still do most of the asking, shy women who rely on men to make the first move may be waiting a long time. Researchers have consistently found that men, when selecting their prospective mates, typically emphasize physical attractiveness. Thus, men (particularly if they are non-shy) tend to be more aggressive in pursuing the small number of women society deems the most physically attractive. Unfortunately, that leaves the rest of the shy female population waiting for a very long time.

But it's not just about a woman's looks; even physically attractive

IF YOU STILL WANT HIM TO MAKE THE FIRST MOVE

What if you're the old-fashioned type who still believes men should initiate romance? If so, you may want to consider this: When you wait for Prince Charming to do the asking, you're severely limiting your choices.

Consider the possibility that the man you like is shy and very cautious about coming on to you; if you could only break the ice, he would be yours. Or perhaps your top choice is the guy who is still hurting over his last relationship, and he's superreluctant to introduce himself to another potential "pain giver." Or how about the possibility that your prospective man-sweet is so tired, preoccupied, or busy that he just doesn't notice you? If he's the One, you may be missing out if you sit back on your shy side and hope he'll approach you.

Now that you've unwittingly succeeded in eliminating most of the desirable men from consideration, who's left? That's right—the aggressive, game-playing men who are willing to keep approaching you until you say yes. Unfortunately, many of these men are less interested in building a lasting relationship than in scoring points on their romantic scorecards. For them mating is a hunt, and you are the prey.

The solution? Learn how to subtly and confidently approach the men you really want to meet, in your own shy-sensitive way. When you combine your shy side with your assertive side, you will greatly increase your dating opportunities and open yourself up to fun and exciting romantic adventures.

women are spending more time next to silent telephones. Shy men have always been reluctant to make the first move, and even non-shy men are more wary of being rejected in the sexual harassment, AIDS-conscious world we live in today. Therefore, more men—both shy and non-shy—are laying back and waiting for women to do a lot of the dating work.

An interesting study found that two-thirds of the American women observed in bars initiated the pickups and conversations with men by enticing them with coquettish looks, questions, compliments, and jokes. This confirms the well-supported idea that women, not men, are actually the ones making the first move. Women usually jump-start the courtship by signaling their preferred men in subtle ways that encourage the men to approach them.

Many shy men and women, however, still cling to the old-fashioned notion that it's the man's job to break the ice. As a result, both suffer from their erroneous assumptions: Shy men become extraanxious because they mistakenly think they have to make the first move all the time, and shy women handicap themselves by waiting for the man to make the first approach, which he usually doesn't do anyway.

The bottom line is that shy women today are in the same boat as shy men. Both need to learn subtle, creative, and shy-sensitive ways to break the ice, create sparks, and develop intimate relationships.

Shyness and Culture: How Do You Say *Shyness* in Japanese?

Michiko, a twenty-nine-year-old Japanese foreign exchange student, had a hard time understanding American culture. Some Americans seemed so rude, so pushy. In Japan you listened carefully to your friends, and you reserved your speech for important matters. All this talk, arguing, conflict—she was surprised that Americans could keep their friends with so much disturbance. Although she loved much about her adopted country, she still couldn't understand American social ways.

In Japan she was respected for being modest, quiet, humble, and shy. But here she felt looked down upon because she didn't talk much in class, because she didn't go out of her way to start conversations and make friends. Here her shyness seemed like a handicap that prevented her from being truly accepted. She wondered what she had to do to be socially valued and loved in America.

Imagine a culture where almost everyone is quiet and shy. Not only are a majority of people shy but shyness is accepted and even embraced by the mainstream. Such a society may not yet exist on earth, but some countries, including Japan—in contrast to the Western world—appear to have a much more accepting attitude toward people who are considered quiet, sensitive, and shy. In Finland, for example, there is a saying: "He who speaks much, knows little. Speak less, think more. A loud voice shows an empty head."

In Shanghai, China, children who are shy or quiet are also considered good, well-behaved, sensitive, and understanding. Researchers compared Shanghai second- and fourth-graders with an equivalent group of children in Canada. They found that in China (unlike in Canada) children who were described as shy and sensitive were among the most preferred as playmates and friends. The shy children in the study were the most desired by their peers precisely because they were quiet and sensitive.

In Japan the societal focus is on maintaining group harmony. Traditional Japanese would rather experience silence than risk disturbing the community equilibrium with negative or idle talk. Because Japanese don't want to say the wrong thing, they say little and let their actions speak for them.

On the positive side, this mind-set encourages the development of people who are sensitive and subtle. Because Japanese speak softly, subtly, and sparingly, both speaker and listener must be especially attuned to each other to fully understand each other's meaning. Communication then becomes a lovely art form in which two people are fully engaged in its intricacies.

Now compare the traditional Japanese style with the Western approach of "I'm louder than you; I'm better than you" verbal confrontations. In the Western one-upmanship style, the person who speaks loudest and fastest, who gets in the last word, and who can outlast and outargue the other person wins the debate. The loser goes down in defeat.

When it comes to dating, the aggressive non-shy Western approach may resemble a boxing match. Expressions such as "hit on," "come on," "hook up," "make a move," and "score" are part of the dating vocabulary and speak loudly of win-lose dating encounters punctuated by lies, loud words, and hurt feelings. No wonder many men and women complain about the deceitfulness, insensitivity, and aggressiveness of the dating world today.

If the Western concept of dating doesn't appeal to you, you might wonder what it's like to live in a country like Japan. You may even be thinking: Shouldn't I just pack up, move to Japan, and date there?

Not necessarily. Although the traditional Japanese social system has certain advantages, it also has its drawbacks. One potential pitfall is that Japanese are reluctant to confront a new friend or dating partner because they're afraid of damaging and losing the relationship. Rather than acknowledge and handle conflicts as they arise, Japanese go around the issue and, in the process, build up hidden tension and resentment.

If there's a problem, Japanese first engage in a subtle form of pre-confrontation by dropping hints that something is wrong. If the problem continues, the dissatisfied partner may engage in the last resort: a confrontational blowup in which he or she expresses everything in a heated and emotional manner. This is risky business, because if it gets to this point, there's a fifty-fifty chance that the relationship will be destroyed forever. And once Japanese end a relationship, they find it extremely difficult, if not impossible, to revive it. Once it's gone, it's usually gone forever.

Another potential drawback is that Japanese are often unsure of where they stand in a relationship. Because much of their communication is subtle and directed through third parties (Japanese will test the waters first by asking friends if the other person is interested in them), a guessing game often ensues. For a long time Japanese may not say anything to their love objects but may spend a lot of time thinking: Does he really like me? Should I say this or do that? Consequently, they may suffer from wasted time and energy, misunderstandings, and hurt feelings if the person they're interested in turns out to be not so interested or not so interesting.

Finally, when shy Japanese come to Western countries, or if they're born into those societies as second- or third-generation descendants, they, too, must learn how to integrate their quiet, reflective, and subtle upbringing with the more assertive, outgoing, and direct social style preferred by the West.

The best way to having a successful shy dating life, therefore, lies in merging the Eastern and Western approaches and learning how to integrate your shy-sensitive personality with the Western values of extraversion, assertiveness, directness, and verbal communication.

When you do this you will have the best of both worlds, and you'll be able to find romantic satisfaction and love wherever you go.

Toward a Shy World Society

Isaac, a shy, thirty-eight-year-old electrical engineer, has friends coming over tonight. Well, not exactly coming over. He's going to have one of his monthly cyber parties with three of his best friends in the whole world: Giovanni from Italy, Maria from Argentina, and Elsa from Germany. They'll meet on the Web and enjoy each other's company—chatting, playing cyber games, and having a blast all night long. His geographically proximate friends, Alex and Betty, will come over during the weekend. With Isaac and his primary partner, Evelyn, they will spend a relaxed, intimate evening, talking, drinking wine, and laughing at the latest comedy videos.

Except for work and shopping, Isaac rarely leaves home, but he can't imagine a better or more fun social life. Even though some people call him shy or reclusive, he doesn't care. he never regrets the old days, when he used to schlepp to Manhattan and fight the traffic, crowds, and insanity just to have a fun night out.

Now things are easier. Home entertainment is in, and he loves the way his social life is structured. He wishes other people could experience the same privacy and comfort he enjoys with his wonderfully loving and supportive partner and friends.

As people continue to cram into urban centers, we will increasingly become a society of privacy seekers and home comfort dwellers like Isaac. We will become more selective about the people we allow into our lives, and we will seek to create a secure, comfortable, home-based social life that insulates us from crowds, pollution, crime, and other nuisances in the environment. Technology will further this trend by giving us the freedom, flexibility, and convenience to connect with people from the privacy of our homes.

As we live more private and inward lives, so will our children and their children. Shyness rates will continue to increase in the twenty-first century, and in the near future we may be living in a world of predominately shy people. Is that bad? Not at all. As long as we eliminate the stigma attached to shyness, this will be a positive social development. As we become more of an inwardly focused society, our collective level of social sensitivity will increase. We will reflect more upon ourselves and the nature of our relationships, and we will be more empathetic. We will spend more time nurturing the few important relationships in our lives, and we will treat the rest of the people on earth in a gentle, sensitive, and compassionate manner.

Wait a minute, aren't you forgetting something? ask the more outgoing members of the population. If we became a world of shy people, we would also be a lonely, isolated society where no one talks to anyone. Where we all live in our plastic cocoons staring at computer screens, without any real human contact.

Nonsense. Repeat after me: Shy people love human contact. There is nothing in the world that a shy person wants more than to make friends, socialize, and create loving and lasting relationships. In fact, shy people crave human contact so much that they often let their emotions get out of hand when they think about the scary-exciting prospect of meeting someone new.

One of the biggest complaints many people—shy and non-shy alike—have is that they have superficial contact with a large number of people in their urban communities, but little real human connection. In the course of a day they may come into contact with dozens of people, none of whom could really be called a friend.

Shy people, perhaps even more than non-shy individuals, crave intimate personal relationships. Rather than settle for superficial encounters with many people, shy people want to invest their emotional energy in a few close friends—and one loving partner—for life. As long as they can prevent their powerful emotionality and intense self-reflection from getting in the way, shy people can successfully cross the bridge to intimacy and meet the few people they need to create and sustain compatible, lasting relationships.

The shy world of the twenty-first century, therefore, would not be a lonely, isolated one. It would be a cozy, comfortable one in which shy people would enjoy their mates and small enclaves of trusted friends, acquaintances, and family members. Wasteful small talk, forced alliances, fake smiles, empty parties, and superficial social interactions would be things of the past.

People would listen more to each other and truly understand each other's positions. Words would be used wisely, and silence would be highly valued as a versatile communication tool that can express a depth of love mere words cannot. Lovers would be more attuned to each other's nonverbal needs, and men and women would respect and love each other in a shyly tender way, devoid of pretense, one-upmanship, and power and control issues.

This all sounds so perfect, so utopian, but it can happen. With the right mix of awareness, knowledge, and personal growth, shy people can begin to build a society that respects and reveres their contribution to the world.

But before we get to this heady shy social world, we still have a lot of work to do. We first need to completely demolish the stigma associated with the word *shyness* and begin to recognize the positive real-world traits that shy people possess by virtue of being shy. Once we do this, we can begin to see shyness as the tremendously powerful advantage it really is. Used intelligently, the Gift of Shyness will reward you with an enriched social life, a deeply satisfying love relationship, and a contented heart and mind. Get ready now to receive your true inheritance: the Gift of Shyness.

CHAPTER 3

The Seven Gifts
of Shyness

David, a thirty-two-year-old patent attorney, was at his rope's end. Shy, never married, and desperately lonely, he had dated infrequently over the past several years and had never really had the loving, committed relationship he had always wanted. He knew there was only one person who could help: his best friend, Bob, a successful shy accountant and father of four who had been happily married for the last ten years to Alice, one of the most beautiful and kind women David had ever known.

When David arrived at Bob's house, Bob immediately knew something was wrong with his usually upbeat and confident friend. "I have to tell you something, Bob," began David in a soft mumble. "I've never said this to anyone, but here it is: I'm a dating loser. I'm just a shy klutz when it comes to women, and I don't know what to do about it."

Bob looked at his friend and considered his plight carefully. "Maybe you're right," he said in his best deadpan voice. "You're definitely a quiet man, way too quiet to meet women."

"Wait a minute," replied David with a hint of irritation. "I may be quiet, but I'm a good listener. Some women like that."

"True," replied Bob, grateful that David had taken the bait. "But you spend a lot of time in your own head. How's *that* going to impress women?"

"What are you talking about?" asked David with increasing energy. "Women are attracted to men who are deep. You know I'm not just some superficial Joe."

"No, you're not," replied Bob. "But how do you expect to meet women when you have only a couple of friends? Where's your social life?"

"Are you kidding?" asked David. "You have only me and Jack, and you found a great woman. I like having a few close friends, for life, that's just me. You know I'm loyal."

"But your feelings get hurt so easily," said Bob, really enjoying himself now. "How can you maintain a relationship like that? You're way too sensitive."

"Maybe I am," replied David. "But I care deeply about people. I'm passionate about relationships. What's wrong with that?"

"Nothing at all," said Bob, as he let his hidden smile break through. "In fact, it's all good—everything you've just told me: You're a deep man who is also loyal, not to mention sensitive and caring. That's the kind of stuff that really turns women off, isn't it, David?"

For the first time in a week, David smiled. The smile turned into a big grin, then laughter, as he realized what his friend was doing. "I'm shy and all those things too," said a beaming David. "I have a lot to offer the right woman, don't I, Bob?"

"Yes, you do," replied Bob as he offered David a glass of red wine to celebrate his new perspective.

It's a shame that a lot of people, including many shy individuals, don't truly appreciate the Gift of Shyness. They don't recognize all the beautiful and wonderful qualities that shy people possess. Rather than celebrate the arrival of a shy-sensitive person into the world, many people lament the birth of another social cripple.

Yet despite what the majority of society may think, things are about to change. We are going to shatter society's misguided views and show you how to own the incredible Gift of Shyness by examining the seven smaller gifts that shyness encompasses—sensitivity, faithfulness, listening ability, reflection, modesty, mystery, and gentleness.

Although you probably possess these traits in abundance, you may not know how to use them to your advantage. In this chapter you will learn to embrace and enhance your shy gifts so you can achieve better dating results than ever before.

The Gift of Sensitivity

All her life Meredith, a thirty-four-year-old redheaded nurse, had known she was sensitive and shy. Little things—a person's tone of voice, the way someone looked at her—affected her deeply. Harsh words from someone she loved or respected could turn her into an emotional wreck for days. In the past Meredith had kicked herself for being so vulnerable. She lamented her thin skin and fragile mind-set and wished she could be a lot tougher.

After she learned about her shy gift of sensitivity, however, Meredith's attitude changed. She started to realize that this side of her personality had admirable elements that could enhance her social life and help her find her soul mate. With her newfound confidence Meredith joined a dating club and eventually met her ideal man: Roger, a non-shy, forty-two-year-old, sandy-haired mechanic. He wasn't as sensitive as Meredith, and he sometimes put his foot in his mouth. But he loved what she brought to the table—her kind and empathetic ways, her sweet and giving nature.

And Meredith enjoyed the balance created by having a more straightforward and aggressive partner like Roger, who was comfortable arguing over the restaurant bill if necessary. Together, they made a perfect yin and yang; each accepted and loved what the other contributed to the relationship.

Now, after two years of bliss, Meredith and Roger are looking forward to spending the rest of their lives together as husband and wife.

There is no greater romantic gift than sensitivity: the ability to absorb the essence of other people and respond to them on a deep emotional level. Many shy people overflow with this type of sensitivity and are able to feel deeply for others. Because shy people are so sensitive, they tend to have fragile, delicate natures that can be easily hurt if they don't protect themselves from critical people or harsh environments. At the same time shy people have an extraordinary gift for turning their sensitivity outward to care deeply for others.

Western society, unfortunately, has seldom recognized the value of shy-sensitive people. Eastern society, by contrast, has had a much more embracing attitude toward those who are considered shy. For example, in a study with second- and fourth-grade Chinese children, researchers found that shy-sensitive students were accepted among their peers and well-adjusted to the school environment; overall, they had a healthy level of self-esteem. Moreover, teachers viewed the shy-sensitive students as competent, and these students tended to receive many leadership and honor positions in the school. Finally, the shy-sensitive children continued to perform well in school, suggesting a positive long-term connection between shyness-sensitivity and social and academic success among these students.

This study demonstrates that people can be shy-sensitive and still possess a rock-solid sense of competence and self-esteem. Although others may not understand them, the key is for shy-sensitive people to embrace their nature and remind themselves that the more shy-sensitive they are, the more desirable they'll be as romantic partners.

Shy people can offer their mates extraordinary empathy—putting themselves in their partners' shoes and seeing life as they see it. Because many shy people have been social underdogs most of their lives, they know what it's like to feel isolated, lonely, and cast aside. They can identify with, and truly feel for, other people, especially those who have been abused, hurt, discriminated against, and rejected by society because they were different.

Moreover, shy people have a heightened sense of self-reflection—and a strong Observer—which makes it easy to see themselves through the eyes of another person. Since shy people are already perceiving themselves from the other person's perspective, they can opt to stay inside that person's head and feel what he or she is experiencing. The strong sense of empathy shared by shy people also tends to make them highly conscientious. They know how others would feel if they let them down because it would be like letting themselves down. Shy people, therefore, take special pains to do what they promised, and do it well.

Being sensitive and empathetic can work wonders in romantic relationships. Imagine what it would be like if your honey knew precisely how you were feeling just by gazing into your eyes. As soon as you walked in the door after a terrible day at work, your partner would know exactly what you needed. He or she would make you the perfect margarita, put on your favorite classical guitar CD, and prepare your scented oil bubble bath, just the way you like it.

If this sounds like something you would do for your mate, realize this: There are a lot of terrific people out there who would give anything to have a sensitive person like you as their romantic partner. You're the one who can make your mate feel like the luckiest person on earth.

Loving the Gift:
The Sensitivity-Enhancing Exercise

For the next ninety days use your gift of sensitivity to enhance your social encounters. Here's how you can do it.

STEP 1. Find a friend and ask him or her to help you with a non-verbal communication experiment. Before you meet, write down a list of questions you would like answered, such as these:

1. *How is my friend feeling right now?*
2. *How is my friend feeling about his or her relationship?*
3. *How is he or she feeling about work?*
4. *What can I say to lift my friend's spirits right now?*

STEP 2. As you sit with your friend, tell this person that neither of you will say anything for the next several minutes. Now pull out your list of questions and focus on "feeling" the answers based on the vibes you're picking up. Write down what you feel for each question. For example, in answer to question 1, you might write: "Judy is feeling sad," or "Sad." Go through the list of questions until you have written either an answer or "no answer."

STEP 3. Check out your answers with your friend. You may be surprised to discover that you were quite accurate.

With your sensitive nature as a starting place, you can eventually become quite good at picking up on someone's emotional state and discerning how this person really feels. You can even try this with people you don't know very well and turn it into a fun icebreaking game. For example, after being introduced to an interesting person at a cocktail party, you might say: "I have the feeling that something really good happened to you today, and you still feel like celebrating the news."

As you hone your gift of sensitivity, people will be amazed at how easily and accurately you can read their true feelings. Some will be so fascinated that they will be attracted to you like magnets to steel. Others will be clueless and won't fully understand just how special you are. Never mind. You will reserve your gift of sensitivity for those who truly appreciate what you have to offer and who can give you something marvelous in return.

The Gift of Long and Loyal Relationships

"If you want a faithful man, marry a shy man. He has few opportunities to cheat, and he will be happy with one good woman." This practical advice was given to Marisol by her mother, Esperanza, and it had served her mother well. Esperanza had married a shy mariachi named Juan, and they had been happily married for more than forty years.

Now Marisol was dating Carlos, a shy, curly-haired twenty-seven-year-old accountant, and she was weighing her mother's words carefully. Carlos had never dated in high school or college and had had only one girlfriend before Marisol. But he didn't seem to crave more dating experiences; he said he loved Marisol, and he wanted to settle down and start a family.

Marisol believed him. In all the time she had known Carlos, he had been a man of his word; deep down, Marisol knew Carlos would be a one-woman man. And the more Marisol thought about it, the more she realized Carlos was everything she wanted in a mate—sweet, sensitive, and conscientious. She knew a man like Carlos would be a loving husband and father and would make her extremely happy for life.

As a shy person, you're probably one of the most loyal and faithful partners anyone could have. Because getting into a relationship is not especially easy for you, you're likely to be quite appreciative and grateful when you're able to develop a good one. Therefore, you're more than willing to invest a great deal of time and energy to make a relationship work, and once you choose the right person, you're usually in there for the long run.

Researchers have supported the idea that shy people, compared with non-shy people, tend to be more monogamous and faithful. They have found, for example, that shy people are more likely to be exclusive daters; that is, they date only one person at a time. Shy people are also more selective in their dating habits: They accept fewer blind dates and know their partners much better before dating them.

Overall, there is little support for the commonly held notion that shyness is responsible for relationship problems. In fact, researchers have found that the spouses and long-term partners of shy people tend to see them in a positive light—as sincere, dignified, mannerly, organized, precise, calm, patient, and modest.

In today's HIV-conscious society, it's important to know that a romantic partner is monogamous and faithful. Those who date a shy person can be fairly certain that their partner won't cheat on them. Nothing is 100 percent guaranteed, of course, but the chances are good that a shy person won't risk losing the relationship by cheating on his or her partner. After all, shy people hate the idea of having to go back into the singles world to meet a new partner. They're perfectly content to invest their time and energy in one person who satisfies their deepest desires.

Loving the Gift: The Relationship Time Line Exercise

In this exercise you will become more aware of your long-term relationship patterns, and you will learn how to appreciate the faithfulness and loyalty you bring to relationships.

STEP 1. Go to your desk or kitchen table and sit quietly with your eyes closed. Think of all the close friends and significant romantic partners you've ever had, all the people who have meant something in your life. Try to remember as far back as possible. Perhaps you're able to recall your earliest friend in kindergarten or first grade.

STEP 2. Write down the name of each friend or romantic partner on a separate piece of paper. Then write down as many things as you can remember: the person's age when you met (as well as your age), his or her physical appearance and personality, how you met, where you met, how long you were together, how you felt about each other, why you stopped being friends or romantic partners (if you did), happy and sad times you shared, and activities you did together.

STEP 3. Create a time line that chronicles each major relationship you have had at every point in your life.

Begin by drawing two circles at the top of a blank sheet of paper, one on the left side, one on the right. In the left-hand circle write your age when you met your first friend. In the right-hand circle write your friend's name and his or her age at the time. Now draw a line between the two circles. Above the line write the period of time you were friends (ten years, twenty years, and so forth).

Go a little farther down the page and repeat the process for you and the next important friend (or romantic partner) in your life. If the friendship was a romantic one, put a star next to the number of years you spent together. Keep going (and use as many sheets of paper as you need) until you have drawn circles that chronologically represent all your key friendships and romantic partnerships from your earliest memory until today.

Let's say, for example, that you met your first friend when both of you were five, and this friendship has lasted for thirty-five years and is still going strong. Moreover, when you were twenty-two you had your first serious romantic relationship, and that lasted eleven years.

When you do this exercise, you may find that you tend to keep your friends and romantic partners for a long time. As a shy person, you may not have a large number of relationships, but those you do have tend to be meaningful and long-lasting.

The Gift of Listening

"All my life I was the quiet child," said Matt, a twenty-six-year-old hip-hop fanatic who wears his jet black hair in a ponytail and loves skiing, playing chess, and surfing the Net. "In class I was last to raise my hand, but I always managed to be a good student, getting mostly As and Bs.

"In high school I was too shy to date, and I thought I was doomed to be desperate and dateless. Most of my friends were shy nerd types, and between us we couldn't scare up a girl if our lives depended on it.

"After I got out of high school, my social opportunities continued to suck, and I was in a desperate funk. It was then that I decided to volunteer at a twenty-four-hour counseling hot line to see if I could do some good and get out of my rut.

"Man, it was so cool. My shyness didn't make a damn bit of difference because I was there to listen and help people who were really hurting. I knew I was contributing, and it made me feel fantastic; my self-esteem hit the limit.

"I was getting so good at it that other volunteers started to notice because the supervisor would praise my performance all the time. One volunteer who noticed was my favorite, Gloria, a real cutie with killer blue eyes that shined like real dreams.

"One night during a break we started rapping about why teens commit suicide, and before I knew it, she asked me out. She was always the more aggressive one, but I didn't care; I loved it. After three months of dating, we hooked up and moved in together. We're livin' large now and loving it."

Oh, what people wouldn't give to own your pair of ears and have them available anywhere, anytime. You, shy person, are a hot commodity because you excel in the one thing many people lack: the gift of listening. In our twenty-four-hour, talking head, media-dominated society, everybody wants to talk, but how many truly listen?

As a shy person, you love to take in all the information and wisdom people have to offer. If some people talk too much, big deal. Let them tire themselves out if they want to. You'll simply extract the meaningful information and discard the rest.

And guess what? Because you talk less than average, people think you're a better listener, whether you really are or not. In a study of vocal activity and listening ability, researchers found that, in the eyes of others, the more people talked, the less they seemed to listen. For example, those who talked more than average in a group of four (more than 25 percent of the time) were not seen as understanding their conversational partners very well. As a good listener, you may not talk as much as others, but you're certainly in perfect sync with the conversational needs of your partner.

In fact, research shows that you're not just good at listening to the actual words being said, you're also skilled at picking up on the emotional nuances of a conversation. Researchers have found that shy people are sensitive listeners who are able to listen to both the content and the emotional meaning of a message—hearing what was implied but not actually said.

As a shy listener, you can easily use your dynamic listening skills to create rapport, understanding, and connection with the people you're interested in. Once you're in a relationship, your eager ear will absorb your partner's wants, needs, and desires, and help him or her feel truly loved.

Loving the Gift: The Reflective Listening Exercise

Reflective listening is a communication tool that therapists use to establish rapport. You can also use it as part of your dating repertoire. It works like this: When you're conversing with someone, repeat certain key phrases back to the person. Because these phrases are important to your conversational partner, you will demonstrate how much you care about what he or she has to say.

STEP 1. Pick a friend or acquaintance you are very comfortable with and start a conversation. As you listen to your friend, concentrate on being 100 percent attuned to what he or she is saying. Focus not solely on the words but also on the tone of voice, inflections, rate of speech, and nonverbal gestures, such as arching eyebrows, throat clearings, and tightened fists. Be observant, and get a pure ears-eye view of what this person is about. Ask a few questions when appropriate or say a few uh-huhs. Your goal is to let the person talk while you do most of the listening.

STEP 2. Once you've established a good listening flow to the conversation, repeat key phrases back to your partner.

For example, your friend may say something like "I'm really worried about the repairs on my car; it'll probably break my back to pay for them."

You reply with: "Sounds like your back is already broken, worrying about that."

He says: "Yeah, I have too many bills right now. It's tough to be a student and work full-time."

You say: "A full-time working student, it must be tough."

As you repeat the key phrases—"broken back" and "full-time student"—you're showing your friend that you're actively interested in his or her problems and that you want to provide emotional support. You're acting like a good friend, and this person is likely to feel closer to you at the end of the conversation. Since you sincerely care about this person, your reflective listening accurately conveys your true feelings in a powerful way.

STEP 3. As you become comfortable using reflective listening with your friends, try it on someone you'd like to know better. The advantage of this approach is that you don't have to say a great deal or be extremely witty or extraverted to make a good impression. You can simply repeat a few choice words and key phrases that reflect the important things your conversational partner is thinking and feeling.

As you do this, you will find that your careful and active listening, rather than flashy talk or creative repartee, is what brings you closer to people and creates the opening for a nice relationship to blossom.

The Gift of Reflection

Shirley, a shy, forty-three-year-old, never-married African American office administrator, wasn't exactly the petite feminine type. With her five-foot-five, two-hundred-pound frame and husky voice, she could appear intimidating to those who didn't know her very well. Yet Shirley was actually quite shy and sweet, not to mention intelligent and resourceful. Unfortunately, the men around her couldn't seem to look past her exterior to see the large-hearted, loving woman inside.

Although Shirley wanted to find the right guy, she'd be damned if she would spend another night at another meat market bar or tacky singles event. Shirley knew her real worth: She was all that *and* a bag of chips. All she needed was a smart man who could appreciate her big outside and her shy little inside.

Shirley loved to read, and she was a big thinker and dreamer. She especially loved science fiction novels and had always been a big *Star Trek* fan, so she decided to get involved in Star Trek conventions and activities to see if she could have fun and meet some interesting, brainy men who would respect her intelligence.

Shirley ended up having a blast at the conventions and met a lot of interesting people. Because the conventions gave Trekkies the opportunity to dress up and act like *Star Trek* characters, Shirley's shyness didn't bother her as much. She let her inner actress take over as she became a powerful Klingon commander. At her last Star Trek convention, Shirley met Jerome, a six-foot-five, forty-five-year-old electrician who referred to himself as Black Spock and was all decked out in the Spock character, all the way down to gigantic ears.

Jerome loved big ladies like Shirley, and he was captivated by her grasp of scientific concepts and her deep, reflective mind. In turn, Shirley loved Jerome's sassy mouth, sexy eyes, and logical way of thinking. Together they spent many marvelous hours conversing about topics like time travel, life on other planets, and Vulcan mind-meld techniques.

Now Shirley and Jerome are engaged, and they're planning their wedding around the next Star Trek convention. They're two Trekkies in love.

You, shy person, are the deepest of thinkers. As a thoughtful, complex person, you don't simply see things for what they appear to be. You probe deeper, analyzing the paradoxes of life and using your formidable intellect to come up with new ideas, systems, and approaches. Some people might call you self-absorbed, but you're really living in a different kind of world—your thought kingdom—an empire as vivid, as real, and as powerful as anything that exists on the outside.

When it comes to relationships, you put a lot of thought behind your choices. You're not the type of person who takes relationships on casually; you realize that each person you allow into your life will use up more of your treasured private time and social energy. Because of this you're likely to take your time deciding whether someone fits into your long-range relationship plans. If this person is the right one, you will do everything possible to make him or her happy. And once you commit to a partner, you will probably stay with that person for life.

As a reflective shy person, you have a lot to offer your mate. You can provide a fresh perspective to help your partner see the world in a unique and fascinating way. And you can keep your mate intrigued and entertained with your deep conversations about science, the arts, business, politics, and anything else that stimulates your remarkable intellect.

Loving the Gift: The Conversational Topic Exercise

In this exercise you will learn how to use your natural intellectual ability to bone up on several interesting topics before you hit the social scene. As a shy person, you will feel more comfortable and secure if you know you have a few pet topics in reserve to keep the conversation going whenever it starts to drag. Use these ready-made topics as conversational lubricants anytime you're in the presence of that alluring stranger. Here's what you can do.

STEP 1. Go to the library and peruse several books and magazines on interesting topics you would enjoy discussing. Write down or remember as many interesting facts and details as you can.

STEP 2. The next time you find yourself in a conversation with an attractive person, mentally pull out your list of preplanned topics and be prepared to discuss several of them. You can transition into your desired topics by finding out what your new friend is interested in, then gradually move into your areas of expertise.

You can, for example, ask your friend what he likes to read in his spare time. If he says self-help psychology, you can ask questions about his favorite authors and topics. Then you can segue into talking about your favorite psychologist, perhaps Carl Jung, and specifically your preferred topic, the collective unconscious—how all of us share certain unconscious universal images that are passed down by our ancestors and give us wisdom for daily living.

STEP 3. Once you're comfortable starting conversations with your preselected topics, you can work on extending your comfort level to topics you're not as familiar with.

As you spend more time with others in the social world, you will realize that your deep, reflective mind is a highly prized attribute that will help you stand out as a truly fascinating person.

The Gift of Modesty

Billy, a twice-divorced thirty-one-year-old stockbroker, had his eye on Martha, a full-figured twenty-five-year-old secretary at his office. Although she wasn't as physically attractive as some of the other secretaries, Martha had a quality Billy found irresistible.

Maybe it had something to do with her soft-spoken, humble nature. She wasn't like many of the other women at the office, always talking about themselves, going on about what they wanted to buy, what they wanted to wear, who they wanted to date. When the gossip mill heated up, Martha pretty much kept to herself. She would listen politely, but she wouldn't get involved or pass judgment.

Yet Martha was always there for her friends. She didn't demand front-page credit for her benevolence; she just seemed to get a lot of satisfaction from helping people in her own quiet way.

Billy knew he had a winner here. She was shy, that was true, and he had to tread carefully so as not to scare her off. But Billy realized she was definitely worth the effort. She was wife material, no doubt about that.

Although they may not make the headline news, many shy people go about their business quietly, helping others on a personal and community level, lending an ear to those who need to be heard and a helping hand to those who need a lift. And through it all shy people will minimize their contributions and, if possible, keep them secret.

When it comes to relationships, modestly shy people are exceptionally hard workers who continually strive to make their partners happy. Unlike people who take their partners for granted as the relationship ripens, shy people continue to do the little things that won their partners' love: the intimate conversations, special nights out, and surprise gifts.

At first glance the modestly shy person may look like a pushover. Some people might even ask: "What's wrong with you? You're way too nice. You're letting John (or Betty) walk all over you. Why don't you demand credit where credit is due?"

Don't be fooled: Just because someone is a modestly shy person doesn't mean he or she is weak-minded. On the contrary: Modesty can be a great source of psychological and social strength. As long as they know their limits, and let others know when they're violating them, shy people can be confidently modest in a way that demands respect. If, for example, you continually do favors for your partner, and he or she doesn't offer anything in return, you can stand firm and say: "Show me respect, or I'm out of here."

Although you can be tough-minded when you need to be, most of the time you will let your quiet modesty speak for you. As a result, you will find yourself excelling in the dating game—shining far brighter than many of the loudmouthed, egotistical, and self-centered people out there. While you're being your modest self, don't think for a moment that you have to be a plain Jane or simple Jack. You can still be an interesting, funny, and exciting date; you can still dress sharp and exude charisma and style.

The difference between you and the dating pretenders out there is that your self-worth is not based on what others think of you, or on how much attention society thinks you deserve. You feel good about yourself because you give to others quietly in a way that embodies grace, dignity, and humility. With your sincerity you say to the world: "I'm just a regular, down-to-earth human being. Would you like to know me better?"

Loving the Gift: The Modesty in Action Exercise

In this exercise you will learn how to accentuate your gift of modesty and make a positive impact on others.

STEP 1. Before you go out each day, remind yourself that you will practice humility in everything you do. You will still feel self-confident and worthy, but you will feel that way from the inner core of who you are, not because you puff your ego up or allow others to puff it up for you. You will wear modesty like a badge that announces, "No one is better than anyone else; we're all equally human."

STEP 2. When you're out in the world, notice how often people try to build themselves up to impress others. Recognize the silly brags, false boasts, and needless exaggeration of their virtues and accomplishments. Realize how unattractive people are when they try to build themselves up just to make a good impression.

Also notice when you're tempted to defend yourself or make yourself seem better than you really are. These are the moments of truth, when you need to take a step back and say things like "Yes, it was my fault. You deserve the credit. I didn't do that much to make it work. I'm not perfect." You don't say these things to diminish yourself, but to reclaim your power as a modest person. Others will respect you more—and will be more attracted to you—when they see how confidently modest you are. The stronger a person is inside, the more modest he or she can be outwardly because there is no need to prove anything to anyone.

STEP 3. Start a Modesty Journal, in which you write down your daily experiences with modest and immodest people. Note how you reacted to them and how others reacted. Also write down those times when you were humble and those times when you allowed your pride to take over. Record your feelings and thoughts at the time and how other people responded to you.

When you become aware of how modesty and pride work in social relationships, you will understand the power and appeal that a genuinely modest person has. You will also be able to detect fake modesty (when people try to appear modest just to make a good impression), and you will strive to be a truly modest person who is comfortable just being you.

The Gift of Mystery

All his life Max had felt different. Quiet and studious, Max excelled in school but pretty much kept to himself, with no real friends except his books. Throughout his college years and later in his job as a chemical engineer, Max wanted to make friends and have lovers, but he felt too shy to excel in the social world. During college he discovered he was more attracted to men than to women, but he still felt unable to do anything about it.

Part of the problem was that Max hated his looks—at six feet three and 170 pounds he had always thought he was too skinny, and he had bad acne scarring left over from his teenage years. To make matters worse, Max had a slight stutter that crept up every time he was around someone in whom he was interested. With all these things going against him, Max thought it was better to stay home and avoid the pain of rejection.

Finally, at twenty-eight, Max decided he was fed up, and he started working with a shyness coach. Doing a complete makeover, Max dropped the tight clothes he had been wearing and began favoring stylish baggy pants, fedoras, and high-heeled boots. His color of choice: all black. His message: "I'm mysterious, sexy, and alluring; come and meet me."

After several weeks of hanging out at coffeehouses and bars with his new style, Max met Mr. Right in Chad, a handsome, thirty-five-year-old art gallery owner with long black hair and intelligent eyes. Chad was immediately attracted to Max's quiet, mysterious presence, and he found him a refreshing change from the pushy, loud-mouthed men he had been running into lately. Max was equally attracted to Chad and accepted his offer of a drink and conversation.

Max and Chad's friendship blossomed quickly as they discovered how much they had in common (Chad had also been an intellectual loner type in high school). They've been together for six months now, and their relationship is growing stronger day by day.

When you meet someone you like, how much do you tell that person about yourself? Do you disclose everything up front, or do you reveal very little and present yourself as a private and mysterious person? Or perhaps you take the middle ground and reveal certain basic information about yourself while holding back on the more important stuff until later.

Self-disclosure is a popular term in psychological circles. It refers to the process of getting closer to someone by revealing your innermost thoughts and feelings until you've developed a deep sense of trust, intimacy, and love.

While self-disclosure is an important part of any relationship, it can easily be misused when a person goes overboard and discloses too much, too soon: "Yes, I'm recently divorced, and my shrink tells me I need to overcome my fear of commitment, and by the way, what are you doing Saturday night?" By engaging in this type of mega-self-disclosure, some singles start a relationship on the wrong foot. Instead of drawing people closer, they project a sense of desperate neediness that scares them away.

As a shy person, you're unlikely to open your heart so quickly. Chances are, you go the other way: You're overly protective of your innermost thoughts and feelings, and you keep a tight lid on those secret parts of yourself. You may keep these things hidden because you lack confidence in yourself and you're afraid of losing the other person. You think: "If I reveal everything about myself, she will know exactly what kind of (inadequate, boring, insecure, and so forth) person I really am. Once she discovers the truth, she'll be gone."

Although your hesitancy to share yourself can be a hindrance in developing an intimate relationship, there is a smart way to use your tendency toward privacy. In a dating context you can use your naturally secretive nature to create an aura of mystery, adventure, and fun.

Try this: Rather than answering questions directly in a social setting, sidestep them—not in an evasive manner but in a fun and flirtatious way. When someone asks your name, for example, pause and say nothing, or change the subject with a shy smile. If you do this in the right way (see the following exercise) you will stimulate an intense curiosity and interest in others.

This mystery approach works well because people want what

they can't have. The less you tell others about yourself in the beginning—as long as you do it in a fun and slightly flirtatious way—the
more they will want to know about you, and the closer they will
want to get to you. Your goal is to disclose just enough to create a
sense of trust and intimacy, while still holding back enough to
arouse people's curiosity. If you can create this ideal balance, you
will draw others to you and enjoy more interesting and exciting relationships.

Loving the Gift: The Cultivating a Sense of Mystery Exercise

Here's an exercise to help you project that aura of mystery and
adventure.

STEP 1. Think of a mysterious character you would like to role-
play during a night out. Choose a character you've admired from
TV, movies, or books: a private eye with a shady past, an international jewel thief, a countess on the lam. If you're the imaginative
type, you might want to create your own character. Make up someone with a mysterious past who is also sexily confident and charm-
ingly irresistible. Tonight you will become that person; you will let
him or her inhabit your mind as you project an image of mystery,
flirtation, and fun.

STEP 2. When you arrive at the social event, focus on portraying
your character's sense of adventure and mystery. Rather than instantly blurting out information ("I work in insurance. What do you
do?"), try to make the partygoers work to pry your secret information from you.

If, for example, someone asks your name, switch the subject, or
say something like "They call me many things, what would you like
to call me?" If someone asks what you do for a living, reply with
a mischievous smile, "It's top secret. If I told you, I'd have to kill
you."

Your purpose here is not be evasive or antisocial, but to be teas-
ing, flirtatious, and mysterious. You want the other person either to
ask you again—and this time you'll reveal the true answer—or to respond in an equally playful manner.

Depending on your comfort level, you can do this with strangers, or you may want to develop your skills by first trying it out with friends. As a third option, you can practice in front of a mirror and role-play both the person who asks the question and your response.

If you think you need more practice, check out Part 2 and learn how to use role-playing techniques to express the untapped parts of your personality.

The Gift of Gentleness

Lance, a shy twenty-five-year-old forklift operator, hated sports—the aggressive contact, the meaningless activity, the yelling fans. But his buddies at work always insisted on dragging him along to sports bars and sporting events. "Be social, check out the scene," his co-workers kept urging Lance. "Who knows, maybe you'll bag yourself a girlie and get out of your shell."

Meeting a nice lady was definitely something Lance wanted, but he couldn't stand the sports scene or the way his co-workers disrespected women. Lance revered women, and he hated his co-workers' locker room talk. At the same time, Lance criticized himself for not being manly enough. He thought: If I want to attract women, maybe I should be more aggressive like the guys. Women don't like nice men; they want the bad boys. Isn't that what they say?

When Lance explored this issue in therapy, his therapist encouraged him to try new activities and environments where he could meet women who would appreciate his gentle and caring side. Following his therapist's advice, Lance became involved with a local animal rights group that specialized in helping strays find loving homes. Before long, he met Beatriz, a ravishing long-legged twenty-seven-year-old veterinarian who loved animals and enjoyed Lance's sweet personality. For the first time in his life Lance was with a woman who truly appreciated his gentleness. He was equally attracted by Beatriz's beauty and her desire to eliminate brutality toward all living things.

After getting to know each other, Lance and Beatriz fell in love and got married. Now Beatriz is pregnant, and they're going to call their baby girl Serenity—the perfect name for their perfect child.

If shy people ruled the world, we would undoubtedly have far fewer wars, much less violence, and significantly fewer incidents of mean-spirited, aggressive, and cruel behavior. For the most part shy people are simply incapable of committing gratuitous acts of aggression and violence. Shy people, in fact, are usually the complete antithesis of the aggressive, insensitive individuals who dominate conversations, offend others, and generally act in disrespectful ways. Shy people are usually the sweet ones: the gentle, kind, caring, and good-natured people who can be counted on for a smile, a favor, or a good word.

Research backs up the notion that shy people go out of their way to please. Shy people, particularly shy women, tend to act in ways— smiling and nodding more, interrupting others less, and agreeing with and reinforcing what others say—that convey a nonthreatening attitude of friendliness, politeness, and interest.

Some people, however, mistake a shy person's gentleness for weakness because they don't understand the shy person's true nature. Some think that shy people bow down before others because they're afraid of standing up for themselves. On the contrary, shy people can be strong in their gentleness: standing firm when they need to, being tough when they have to be. But their strongest desire is to treat others with gentleness, kindness, and respect because that is the way they would like to be treated.

As a shy person, you're probably very sensitive to everything in life, and you go out of your way to avoid hurting others because you've experienced the real pain of being hurt in social settings. You especially dislike conflict, and you would like everyone to live peacefully in a harmonious and respectful environment. You may not realize it yet, but you can use your gentle nature as a powerful aphrodisiac to attract a great partner. Your gentle demeanor will put people at ease, and they will see you as a special and desirable person who is far superior to the usual suspects—the pushy, aggressive, and selfish types—who infest the dating world.

Loving the Gift: The Gentleness Expansion Exercise

In this exercise you will become fully aware of your gentleness as you offer it to others.

STEP 1. Before you leave the house, take a few minutes to meditate on gentleness. Sit in a comfortable chair with your arms at your sides and your feet flat on the ground. Take a deep breath to clear your mind. Think of all the gentle things in life: animals like the dove or lamb, people like Mother Teresa or Jesus Christ, and environments like lush, green meadows with birds happily chirping overhead.

STEP 2. Visualize a white fluffy cloud that emanates from these gentle animals, people, and places, and that represents the essence of all that is soft, peaceful, loving, pure, and nonviolent. In your mind's eye, see yourself standing next to these gentle symbols (Mother Teresa, for example) as you absorb their essence. See the fluffy clouds as they float right into your psyche, your soul, immediately calming your mind and bringing you a feeling of peace, acceptance, and goodwill toward everyone on earth.

STEP 3. Go into the world with your attitude of goodwill, and watch yourself as you spread your gentle touch wherever you go.

When you're in a long checkout line on a hot, busy day, for example, visualize that you're sending your fluffy cloud of gentleness toward the harried checkout clerk—soothing and protecting him or her from the stresses of the job. When you're stuck in traffic and people are honking at you, let your state of gentleness blanket you and provide a calm buffer between your emotions and the overactive aggressive natures of those around you.

Practice this exercise daily and you will build a bridge of gentleness and peace that will carry the right person across the desolate sea of singles into your safe romantic harbor.

Watch the Stereotypes— They're Not You

As you ponder your shy gifts, be aware of any negative stereotypes about shyness that you may have believed until now. The sad truth is that for many people shyness has been not a valuable gift but an ugly cross to bear. Parents, teachers, friends, psychologists, and the media—sometimes well-meaning but ultimately harmful—may have infiltrated your mind with unflattering labels that made you feel lousy because you were shy.

The first step in liberating yourself from these self-esteem-crushing stereotypes is to become aware of them. Some may be crammed so far down in your psyche that you may not be able to recall them unless you put your mind to it.

Exercise 1. I'm Shy, and I Want to Die

In the following space write down all the negative and critical words or phrases that you have ever heard applied to shy people. Put a star next to the items *you* used to believe were either somewhat or very true about shy people in general and you in particular.

You may have written words such as

Antisocial	Selfish
Timid	Vain
Fearful	Arrogant
Shrinking	Slow
Cowardly	Stupid
Suspicious	Withdrawn
Distrustful	Social outcast
Secretive	Nerd
Tight-lipped	Wallflower
Egotistical	Mass murderer—sociopath

Did the last item throw you? Was it too extreme? Consider the typical TV newsmagazine show that profiles the latest serial killer or mass murderer: "X never had any friends; he was introverted, shy, antisocial. He killed to ease his loneliness, his isolation." What kind of picture does that paint? An ugly picture of a recluse who's building up resentments, ready to explode at a moment's notice.

Of course, the media neglect to mention the millions of shy people who do no harm and instead do a tremendous amount of good for their communities. These gentle, quiet people aren't profiled and celebrated. All we see on TV are "experts" droning on about the minuscule number of shy or Introverted people who commit horrific crimes as a result of their mental illness or lack of conscience.

Now that you've collected the verbal garbage, it's time to throw it out. Imagine that you're cutting all these words from a newspaper and tossing them in a garbage can. Throw in a match, and watch all the stereotypical words go up in smoke. How do you feel now?

Exercise 2. I'm Shy, and I Can Really Fly

You've just separated yourself from the negative stereotypes associated with shyness. Your next step is to write down all the positive qualities that shy people possess. Again, write as quickly and as much as you can.

You may have written words such as

Sensitive	*Mysterious*
Empathetic	*Loyal*
Reflective	*Smart*
Intelligent	*Respectable*
Trustworthy	*Conscientious*
Good listener	*Gentle*
Modest	*and so on*

Each week reread all the life-enhancing words you just wrote down; add new ones as they occur to you. Restructure your mental dictionary so you automatically use inspiring, feel-good words when you think of yourself as being shy. Your aim is to counteract the years of propaganda that tried to convince you that you were less than worthy because you were shy.

The Gift of Shyness Is Now Yours

Congratulations. You're already the proud owner of the ultimate social tool: the Gift of Shyness. The greatest thing about this gift is that you don't have to do anything to merit it; you don't have to do anything to earn it. You already have these awesome talents at your fingertips. All you have to do now is apply your shy-sensitive skills in an intelligent and thoughtful manner, and romantic success will be yours.

CHAPTER 4

What Kind of Shy Am I?

When Walter met Suzy in French class, it was love at first sight. She was cute, shy, and sweet, and looked like just the type of old-fashioned girl he had always longed for. And Suzy saw Walter as a good-looking, fun-loving guy who livened up the class with his wacky wit and off-the-wall comments. He seemed like the same kind of party animal guy her dad was, someone she could really have fun with.

As they got to know each other, however, they were surprised to discover the truth: Suzy wasn't really the stay-at-home type at all. She was only shy in the beginning. After she got comfortable in her surroundings, she would want to stay out late and party the night away. Walter, meanwhile, was only "on" for limited periods of time. After he exhausted his social energy, he was dying to go home and recharge by himself with his books and computer.

Realizing how different they really were, Suzy and Walter began to reevaluate their relationship and decided their social styles were not going to mesh. They broke up soon afterward and wondered what went wrong: How could they have so badly misjudged each other's personalities?

When it comes to relationships, what you think you see is not always what you get. The trick is to understand the true personality of the person you're interested in, as well as to really know yourself.

In reality, Walter isn't an outgoing type at all. He's what is known as a non-shy Introvert, someone who is not shy and who, as an Introvert, gets energy primarily from his own thoughts and by spending a lot of quiet time alone. What fooled Suzy, and fools many people, is that a non-shy Introvert like Walter can be quite talkative for a certain period of time. But, unknown to others, Walter can keep up his high-wire social act for only a limited period of time, after which he gets tired and needs to retreat to his private corner of the world.

Suzy, by contrast, is a special breed of shy person: a shy Extravert. Although she's often shy at the beginning of a social encounter, once she gets used to her environment she relaxes and ends up being a social butterfly. As an Extravert she gets her energy primarily from others, and she loves being out with her large circle of friends. Her initially shy, demure nature fools people into believing she is a withdrawn, quiet person when she is anything but.

To Thine Own Self Be True

In my last book, *LoveTypes: Discover Your Romantic Style and Find Your Soul Mate*, I talked about the dating masquerade and how singles put on masks—artificial personas—designed to impress the person they're interested in. The only problem is that once you get to know the person and become comfortable with him or her, the mask comes off, and both of you may realize you are much different—and much more incompatible—than you initially thought.

The quiet man who loves his home-cooked meals and videos becomes a raging party animal to get on his honey's good side. After they're married he reverts to his true tendencies, and she has two words for him: couch potato. The talkative, outgoing woman who loves socializing with her wide circle of friends plays Suzy Homemaker in the initial dating stage, catering to her private man's home-based needs. Once they're married she starts going with her friends for girls' nights out, and he has one label for her: tramp.

To form successful relationships you need to recognize and accept yourself for who you really are, and you need to show that true self to everyone you meet. At the same time, you need to recognize the true nature of those you encounter so you can avoid being blinded by the glitzy image of an attractive face or appealing personality.

Determine Your Social Style with the Shy Type Quiz

Your social style or shy type is your unique way of interacting with people in social settings. It will dictate the types of people you're comfortable with, the kinds of leisure activities you enjoy, how you initiate (or don't initiate) romance, how you get (or don't get) your sexual needs met, the sorts of relationships you'll have, and much more.

In the following quiz you will discover your shy type. As you go through the questions, you may see yourself in both answers depending on the circumstances. If so, you need to decide which sentence best describes you *most* of the time; which side do you *tend* to lean on?

1. **I tend to draw more energy from**
   - (E) other people.
   - (I) my own thoughts.

2. **When I'm at a social gathering, I tend to get more energy**
   - (E) toward the end of the night, and once I get going I may be the last person to leave.
   - (I) toward the early part of the night, and then I get tired and want to go home.

3. **Which sounds more appealing?**
   - (E) Going with my date to a place where there are lots of people and social interaction, such as nightclub or party
   - (I) Staying home with my date—watching an entertaining video and eating my favorite take-out food.

4. **When I'm on a date, I'm usually**
   - (E) quite talkative throughout.
   - (I) more quiet and reserved until I feel comfortable.

5. **In the past I have tended to meet most of my dates**
   - (E) when I'm doing things in the outside world: at parties, nightclubs, work, recreational activities, chance meetings, or when friends introduce me to their friends.
   - (I) through private methods, such as personal ads, video dating, and the Internet, or sometimes by introductions from close friends and family.

6. I tend to have
    (E)   many acquaintances and many (or a few) close friends.
    (I)   a few close friends and/or a few acquaintances.

7. In the past my loved ones and partners tended to say this about me:
    (E)   "Can't you be quiet and still for once?"
    (I)   "Can you come out of your shell, please?"

8. I consider myself a shy person in dating situations.
    (S)   Yes, mostly.
    (NS) No, rarely.

9. When I see someone I'm attracted to, my first impulse is to
    (S)   avoid or move away from the person—I'm too nervous.
    (NS) get to know him or her.

10. I'm able to start a conversation easily with someone I'm strongly attracted to, even if I don't know the person very well.
    (S)   Not usually.
    (NS) Most of the time.

11. I feel comfortable at parties or social situations where I'm likely to meet new and attractive people.
    (S)   Not too often.
    (NS) Most of the time.

12. If I'm called upon to speak before a large group of important people, I
    (S)   tend to get tense and nervous.
    (NS) am usually relaxed, confident, and prepared to make a great presentation.

13. When I'm introduced to someone I really like, I
    (S)   may blush, experience an accelerated heartbeat, or have a queasy feeling in my stomach.
    (NS) will usually feel fine, composed, and relaxed.

14. When I meet an intriguing stranger, I'm likely to
    (S)   shy away and wait for him or her to make the first move.
    (NS) take the initiative immediately and express my interest in getting to know him or her better.

Scoring

Add up your answers (count the number of I's, E's, S's and NS's) and place the numbers in the following corresponding spaces. Then circle the two letters (or letter combination in the case of NS) that had the higher scores.

E   I   S   NS

—   —   —   —

Your Shy Type

Now write the letters representing your two highest scores. You are a

—   —

The letters stand for

E—Extravert: You tend to get a majority of your energy by spending time with other people in the outside world.

I—Introvert: You prefer to get energy from your own thoughts and enjoy spending quiet, private time at home.

S—Shy: You're quite sensitive to the social world, and you have a strong Observer that criticizes you and makes you feel self-conscious and vulnerable in social situations.

NS—Non-Shy: You have a relatively thick skin in social encounters, and don't have an overly active Observer.

As an Extravert

- You like to go out and socialize.
- At social events you get more energy as the night progresses.
- You tend to have many friends and/or acquaintances.
- In relationships you enjoy talking a lot and getting everything out in the open.
- You are sociable, outgoing, and group-focused.

As an Introvert

- You like to stay home and think, write, read, meditate, listen to music, or spend time with your computer.
- You go to social events early and typically have less energy as the night progresses. (You often go home early.)
- You tend to have a few long-term close friends.
- In relationships you like to think things over and talk when you're ready.
- You are quiet, inward, and private.

In addition to your letter score, you can determine the relative strengths of each of the dimensions that make up your shy type as follows:

For Shy/Non-Shy and Introvert/Extrovert

4 = Moderate

5 = Significant

6 = Strong

7 = Very strong

Let's say these were your two highest scores:

S	I
<u>4</u>	<u>7</u>

In this case you scored a 4 on S (Shy) and a 7 on I (Introvert). You're a Shy Introvert with a moderate level of shyness (4) and a very strong level of Introversion (7). As a very strong Introvert, you probably get most of your energy from your own thoughts, and you prefer to spend a lot of quality time alone. As a moderately shy person, you sometimes feel uncomfortable in social situations, and you can feel self-conscious in the presence of people you are attracted to. You are, however, not as socially sensitive and self-conscious as those who score higher on the shyness scale.

Keep your dimension scores in mind as you read the rest of this book. If you're borderline on a trait—scored a 4—you may have some characteristics of the opposite trait, and you may need to fine-tune your social plan to match your true tendencies. If you retake this quiz at a later date, your scores may change slightly, although they will probably remain relatively stable over your lifetime.

What's Your Shy Type?

There are no right or wrong answers to the quiz you took; there are no best or worst types. Each type has advantages as well as challenges. Let's examine each of the four types and see where you fit in.

If You're a Shy Introvert

When I first learned about Internet dating, I couldn't believe my luck. I didn't have to go out, talk charming, look perfect. I could just be my shy, quiet self at home, and use my great writing skills to impress the ladies on-line. But honestly, it hasn't worked out; most of the women I've met on-line are not what they seem. I wish I could meet women the old-fashioned way, face-to-face, but I don't think I can.

Shy Introvert, Matthew, computer programmer, 36

You, Shy Introvert, give yourself a hard time when you label yourself inferior because you're shy. You become so concerned about being hurt in social situations that you withdraw from people instead of allowing them the pleasure of getting to know you.

As an Introvert, you can be perfectly content being by yourself at home. Leaving the party early to avoid embarrassment fits in with your natural tendencies to conserve your energy and recharge in private. It takes energy to go out and stay out, and when you're home you can relax. Of course, when you're home you don't meet anyone, and that's precisely the problem.

Another challenge: Because you have a limited amount of social energy, you tend to invest it in a few people. As a result you probably don't have a wide circle of friends and acquaintances who can introduce you to attractive singles and invite you to social events where you're likely to meet your dream mate.

Not only do you have fewer social connections but the friends you do have will probably be Introverted and shy just like you.

INTROVERSION AND EXTRAVERSION: THE TURTLE AND THE RABBIT

Carl Jung noticed that turtles have a strong power of defense—a thick shell—to protect themselves against a potentially hostile environment. In the same way, Jung believed, certain humans have a strong need to insulate themselves from the external world by withdrawing into their thoughts and inner lives. These individuals, whom he called Introverts, tend to have a few close friends and seem to relish their privacy and quiet moments.

Jung also observed that rabbits tend to throw themselves out into the environment and have a much weaker defense against the outside world. Similarly, some people are like rabbits—their primary focus is to seek energy and gratification from the outside world. These individuals, whom Jung called Extraverts, tend to have many friends and acquaintances and enjoy a great deal of social interaction.

In Jung's view neither type was superior; they were simply different. Moreover, each possessed unique advantages.

The Extraverts' advantage lies in their ease in dealing with external matters—people, places, and things. Their outward-focused nature gives them the edge in creating and nurturing social circles that frequently bring them into contact with a large number of people, thereby increasing their odds of meeting a compatible mate.

Introverts, by contrast, have a distinct advantage when it comes to the inner world. Rather than simply seeing the external world as it appears, Introverts look deeper and see the complexity and creativity of life. As a result Introverts can offer their mates fresh insights and dazzle them with their remarkable intellects and probing minds.

Until recently Introverts were the minority in the world—about 25 percent of the population (with 75 percent of people classified as Extraverts). Now, with their ranks rising rapidly due to the influence of the Internet and society's trend toward a more private, home-based lifestyle, Introverts make up approximately 45 percent of the population (with Extraverts a shrinking 55 percent) and will probably surpass Extraverts as the majority before long.

While you're home lamenting the lack of good dating choices, your friends are probably doing the same. Things get worse when instead of going out to meet new, interesting people, you spend Friday and Saturday nights with your friends playing Trivial Pursuit and complaining that all the good ones are taken.

You will have a much happier social life if you redefine your shyness as sensitivity and use it to interact with others in an intelligent and compassionate manner. You will also do well if you get involved in an ideal social structure (you'll learn how to do that in Chapter 12) that enables you to display your fantastic, almost otherworldly virtues—your depth, sensitivity, empathy, thoughtfulness, conscientiousness, loyalty, intelligence, and unbounded creativity—to attract the person you really want to meet.

A reality check first: As a shy Introvert, you tend to face the toughest challenges of any of the shy types. Unless you learn how to use your social style as an asset, you may be hard-pressed to establish a rewarding romantic relationship. That happy, loving marriage or long-term relationship you fervently desire may not materialize unless you transform your Introversion and shyness into a real-world dating advantage.

Beginning with Part 2, you will learn how to develop the Actor-Observer Balance by muting the self-conscious, critical part of your mind (the Observer) while expanding your Actor, the natural and spontaneous part of you. Then, in Part 3 (pay special attention to Chapter 12) you will learn real-world dating approaches and skills that will help you tap into your Introvert and shy attributes to find the love of your life.

If You're a Non-Shy Introvert

People don't really know me—even some of my friends get the wrong impression. Some people think I'm a recluse. Others would swear I'm the most outgoing person they know. Some days I'll just veg out at home, soaking in the hot tub, reading my favorite Terry McMillan novels, or listening to Tupac. Other times, I'm Miss Society: doing nonstop social things, taking off to Vegas with friends, or dancing salsa by moonlight. I'm just weird that way."

Non-Shy Introvert, Vanessa, art student, 24

ARE INTROVERSION AND SHYNESS RELATED?

For many years people have lumped shyness and Introversion together, believing they were one and the same. They thought, If you're shy, you're Introverted. If you're Introverted, you're shy. At first glance this comparison seems to makes sense: Both Introvert and shy people appear to be quiet, private, and retiring individuals who seem more comfortable away from the demands and pressures of the outside world.

Researchers have compared the two factors statistically to see how much they really have in common. They have found that there's a modest inverted connection, or negative correlation, between shyness and sociability. In other words, to a small degree, the more shy a person is, the less sociable (or Extravert) he or she is. This small negative correlation, however, doesn't explain the people who are shy and still sociable, that is, shy and Extravert. Overall, researchers believe that sociability (Extraversion/Introversion) and shyness are separate concepts, although they may overlap a bit.

When examining the trait of shyness, we see that it contains a strong *emotional* component, an ultrasensitivity to the environment that causes the shy person to shrink back in self-protection, and a self-consciousness that makes the shy person criticize himself or herself for being shy. Introversion, by contrast, has a strong *energy* component; the Introverted person withdraws his or her energy from the outside world and carefully conserves it for a few significant social interactions. The best analysis, then, is that, although they share some qualities, Introversion and shyness are actually two distinct personality traits that can have a great impact on an individual's ability to socialize and meet potential romantic partners.

You, non-shy Introvert, are easily the most misunderstood of the shy types. In certain settings, people may see your quiet, reflective side, how you like to spend a lot of time by yourself—reading, writing, thinking, meditating, listening to music, and playing with your computer. Consequently, they may think of you as shy, retiring, and quiet. In other settings people may see you as the life of the party: telling jokes and stories, introducing yourself to new people, and carrying on long, animated conversations. They may think of you as an Extravert, a "never say never" social kamikaze.

So which one are you? The answer is both. Like most people, you have your social side and your quiet, reflective side. However, the more of an Introvert you are, the more likely you are to prefer your more thoughtful, inward style, and the less likely you are to enjoy being around bright lights, loud sounds, and crowded venues.

When people first meet you, they may not understand the real you. They may see your quiet side and think you're shy when you're really not. As a non-shy Introvert, you don't usually have the emotional reactivity of a shy person, and you don't have to go to great lengths to protect yourself from being hurt in social situations. You can be quite sociable and straightforward when you want to be.

When people see your outgoing side, they may still not understand the real you. They don't realize how much you prize your psychological energy, and how carefully you invest it in the right places and with the right people. The more Introverted you are, the less patience you have for blown-up small talk and wasted words. You can hold the conversational fort when you feel it's important or desirable to do so, but you won't keep it up for long if you don't see a strong need for it.

Your dating challenges come in two varieties. First, potential dating partners who see your outgoing side may assume you're a flaming Extravert and may deal with you on that basis. If they're strong Extraverts themselves, they may be disappointed when they realize that, for you, "home sweet home" is not just a trite saying; it is rock-solid truth. A lot of the time you would rather stay home and listen to a good CD than have to fight the crowds, noise, and traffic to hear the same group at a live concert. Your Extravert partner would, of course, argue that listening to the CD is not the same thing as seeing the group live, especially when his or her posse of rowdy friends come along for the ride. Now you have a nice little war on your hands—all because your partner misunderstood your social style from the beginning.

The other challenge you face is meeting people in the first place. This is where you may get really frustrated by well-meaning but misguided friends and family who say things like "I don't understand. You're attractive, charming, and successful. Why can't you meet a nice man (or woman)? I know what's wrong: You need to get out of the house more." No kidding. There's only one little problem: Your home is your castle. And leaving the comfort of your cozy abode to become one of the peons in the dating rat race is not exactly at the top of your wish list. Of course, neither is sitting home alone without a significant other, but then nobody said being an Introvert was going to be easy.

Fortunately, there are many things you can do as an Introvert to jump-start your social life and meet interesting people. First of all, you can apply the ImprovTherapy techniques in Part 2 to develop more of your outgoing, spontaneous Actor and get out of your stay-at-home rut. You can also read Chapter 12 and learn Introvert-friendly dating strategies to help you meet more compatible people and achieve better dating results than ever before.

If You're a Shy Extravert

When I first meet a guy I like, I'm like an old washing machine on double load—I'm shaking all over. If he's nice and we're in a group of mutual friends, I can relax more and eventually get over my shyness. It can take quite a while, but if he gives me the chance, I'll let him know I like him. Then I can really come out of my shell.

Shy Extravert, Alicia, office receptionist, 23

As a shy Extravert, you have more social advantages than an Introvert because you tend to know more people, and you have a better chance of being introduced to Mr. or Ms. Right at a party or social event. As an Extravert, you're also more likely to spend time in the outside world. If, for example, you're a student cramming for an exam, you may enjoy sitting outdoors in a café to soak up the ambience as you hit the books. If a cute guy or gal happens to sit next to you and start a conversation, well, there you are.

Wait, you say. There's one tiny problem. You're shy. That's right. You're a shy Extravert, which is quite an oxymoron to the average person but quite understandable to you. You're shy; therefore, you're especially sensitive and self-protective in social situations where you feel you may be embarrassed or rejected. You also probably possess a strong Observer that makes you feel self-conscious and inadequate in new and threatening social situations.

At the same time you love being out with your friends where all the fun and action are. Although you're usually shy in the beginning, once you get comfortable, you can come out of your shell and become the life of the party. When you're in your groove, no one can stop you: They'll have to zip your lips shut because you enjoy talking and laughing so much.

The Actor-Observer material and ImprovTherapy techniques in Part 2 will be especially useful in helping you get out of your condemning Observer and into your confident, socially successful Actor. You can also take a look at the dating tips in Part 3. There you'll learn how to use your shy-sensitive nature as a real-world dating advantage.

If You're a Non-Shy Extravert

Meeting men is easy; the hard part is finding time to date the ones I'm interested in. My friends are always introducing me to men. I meet men at parties. I even introduce myself to good-looking men at bookstores and coffee shops. I admit it; I'm a die-hard flirt. It's too bad I'm so busy trying to make partner to spend much time dating. So many men, so little time.

                              Non-Shy Extravert, Janice, trial attorney, 44

Of all the shy types you probably have the fewest problems initiating social and romantic relationships. You don't have the self-protectiveness or self-consciousness of a shy person or the limited social energy of an Introvert. You're likely to be outgoing and straightforward, and you're able to create and sustain an extensive social structure that draws a good number of potential romantic partners into your life.

If that's all true, then why are you reading this book? The answer is that you may be moderately non-shy or Extraverted; that is, you're on the border of non-shy/shy or Introvert/Extravert (or both), and you scored 4s or 5s on the Shy Type Quiz. If so, you may share some qualities with shy or Introverted people, and you will benefit from the assistance offered in the rest of this book.

PART TWO

How to Be Shy and Socially Successful

CHAPTER 5

Battling for Your Romantic Life

There she was, his dream girl, shopping alone in a shoe store. She was perfect: tall, shapely, with cute brown hair, clear blue eyes, and deliciously creamy skin—all-American to the bone. Roger, a shy twenty-six-year-old graduate student, couldn't believe his good luck; she was the one he'd been waiting for all his life.

Only one problem: Roger had absolutely no idea what to say to her. He had been in this situation before and had usually blown it—slinking away without saying anything to an attractive woman, then regretting his cowardice for days. This time he had to do something.

"Do you like those?" blurted Roger as he pointed out some shoes Ms. Gorgeous was looking at.

"They're cute," replied Gorgeous. "Do you have 'em in size seven?"

"Uh, size seven?" asked Roger as he frantically tried to think of something to say. He didn't know much about shoes, but he had to have an excuse to talk with her. Fortunately, the real salesman was occupied at the front of the store, and this was Roger's chance.

"I think I can order them," tried Roger. "Can you, er, give me your home phone number so I can call you when they come in?" Roger could swear the whole store was staring at him, the whole world in fact. Still, he had to keep the conversation going, he just had to.

"No, thanks, I'll check the mall," replied Gorgeous as she started to leave.

Be honest, thought Roger. Tell her the truth: I have a confession to make. I don't really work here, I just wanted to meet you. You seem really nice, and I would love to get to know you.

"Thanks for shopping at Roger's Mart, I mean Shoe Mart," mumbled Roger as his beauty walked out of the store. "Come again," Roger called after her feebly, but it was too late. She was out of his life forever. Damn. He had blown it again. Now he was sure everyone in the store would be laughing at him, taunting him: "You're a phony; you're scared to be yourself because no woman would ever want the real you. You're a loser."

Roger could feel the ridiculing eyes of society burning into the back of his head as he made a quick getaway home, where he would feed his fish and snuggle with his dog. At least they would appreciate him.

There's a vicious prizefight going on in your head—a knock-down-drag-out rumble between two feuding mental forces: the Actor and the Observer. These sworn enemies are duking it out to determine who will rule your romantic life. It's a fight to the social death, and the winner takes all.

In one corner stands the Observer, also known as the inner spectator, the final judge. The Observer is the self-conscious part of your mind that's always looking back at you—judging, criticizing, condemning: "How could I look so foolish in front of that attractive person? I'm never going to meet anyone that fantastic again. I'm just a fool."

In the other corner we have the Actor, also known as your spontaneous nature, your authentic self. When your Actor is on top, your natural social talent will shine, and you will be charismatic, attractive, and above all romantically self-confident. The Actor never needs to second-guess itself or worry about making mistakes; it simply acts naturally and lets everything turn out as it may.

The battle over your romantic life hits a fevered pitch when you come across that irresistible person. In one part of your brain you feel the Actor tugging you, imploring, Be yourself, act spontaneous, be a flirt; have some fun. In the other part the Observer is equally vehement in exhorting, Forget about it; you'll be rejected, embarrassed, and humiliated. Go back home to your popcorn and videos.

In the early rounds of this bare-knuckle boxing match, the Observer usually has the upper hand. After all, it has been your closest companion for many years—cleverly incorporating all those critical voices from your past to make you feel inadequate, unwanted, and socially unprepared. The Observer has become the sadistic, tyrannical jailer who delights in keeping you locked up in a prison of fears, self-consciousness, and utter loneliness.

Things may look bleak at the moment, but hope is on the way. Beginning with this chapter, you will learn how to mute the Observer's influence and increase the Actor's power. Before long, the Actor will replace the Observer as the primary force in your social life, and your love life will improve dramatically.

Once the Actor is in complete command, you may ask: Why don't I just wipe out the Observer altogether and live solely from my Actor? Not so fast. Although it's true that the Observer is mostly a negative and destructive influence on your social life, it can also offer you a very important benefit. Used rightly, the Observer can point out any real mistakes you're making and help you correct them. For example, the Observer can tell you when you're speaking too softly, making poor eye contact, or being too hesitant in social encounters. If you listen to the lessons the Observer is trying to teach you, you will make excellent progress in your love life.

It all boils down to developing the Actor-Observer Balance: the perfect combination of Actor and Observer in your personality. Your goal is to have enough Actor to help you respond gracefully and spontaneously in any social situation, and just enough Observer to give you valuable social feedback so you can correct any mistakes.

Unmasking the Observer: Bringing the Enemy to Light

When Katsu, a shy forty-year-old Japanese American biologist, shuffled into my office, I could see the sadness and resignation in his eyes. A virgin until the age of thirty-two, he'd finally had his first lovemaking experience with a paid sexual surrogate and since then had had no significant romantic relationships with women.

I could sense that Katsu didn't just have a strong Observer, he had a cruel, absolute dictator of an Observer.

"My father never said he loved me," began Katsu. "His favorite word to me was *baka* [stupid].

"No matter what I did, it was *baka*. I tried so hard to please him, earning a near 4.0 in high school, but it was never enough. One year I remember, I think I was in ninth grade, I brought home a perfect A report card."

"Did that satisfy him, at least?" I asked.

"No, it didn't," said Katsu with an impassive face. "In return for my perfect grade, he gave me a perfect beating with his belt."

" 'Why are you beating me, Father?' I asked. 'I was perfect today. I brought straight As.'

" 'I am not beating you for today,' said my father. 'I am beating you for the mischief you will get into tomorrow.' "

During our work together Katsu began to realize just how much his father had become his Observer. For years this critical Observer had kept Katsu neutered, convincing him that women would reject him because he was incompetent and unworthy.

Finally, Katsu had a breakthrough that changed everything. On that special day he bounced into my office with a big smile on his face and showed me a beautiful drawing he had made of a mean-looking Samurai warrior. "This was my Observer," he said. "He has tormented me all my life."

"This is a menacing and angry picture, Katsu," I said. "But I notice you're smiling. Why?"

"Because this piece of crap doesn't control me anymore," replied a triumphant Katsu as he crumpled up the fine-crafted drawing and slam-dunked it into the wastebasket.

I was stunned by Katsu's emotion. He had always been like a machine, impassive and unemotional. Now he was alive.

"Katsu, what are you going to do now?" I asked.

"I'm going to meet all the women I haven't met, have all the sex I need, and then find a special woman to love. And I'm going to my father's grave and tell him what's in my heart: " 'The way you brought me up was *baka*. My son will never be brought up the way you raised me, with punishment and pain. He will be treated with love, kindness, and true acceptance. Good-bye, Father. Good-bye, Observer.' "

A child inherits his father's blue eyes, his mother's quick wit. And there's something else that's often passed down from parent to child: the Observer, the storage place for all the negative and critical things that have ever been said about your social abilities. Your parents may have meant well; they may have wanted you to be a socially successful person. But the way they went about it—criticizing, hectoring, and harassing you about your flaws—most likely did you more harm than good. Instead of raising your self-esteem, their critiques became embedded in your mind as the Observer, your lifetime companion from hell.

For some of us, it wasn't our parents but our friends, siblings, teachers, even our own thoughts that became our Observer—the condemning echo that continually reminded us we weren't smart enough, good-looking enough, interesting enough, or worthy enough to capture and hold the affections of the person we really desired.

Yet despite its apparent power, the Observer is not all that tough. In fact, if you look closely, you will realize that the Observer is really a weak entity that must lurk in the dark to do its dirty deeds. The Observer desperately needs to keep a low profile because that is the only way it can survive: by convincing you it doesn't exist, by making you believe its voice is your voice.

When you bring the Observer to the light of your awareness, you will recognize it as the feeble collection of critical voices it really is. Its grip on you will weaken, and you will get your social life in order.

Exercise 1. Give Your Observer a Face

What does your Observer look like? Is it animal or human, male or female? What is its underlying emotion: anger, hatred, or fear? In this exercise you will find out exactly what your Observer is like by putting its image on paper. Of course, when you do this, the Observer is not going to be happy. The Observer is like a criminal who will do anything to avoid being photographed. The Observer knows that once its picture gets out, it won't be able to hide anymore.

STEP 1. Sit quietly with your eyes closed and imagine what your Observer would look like if you saw it in the real world. See the Observer in full detail as it screams, rants, yells, and seduces—trying to convince you that you are unworthy of true love. What does the Observer look like? Sound like? Taste like? Smell like? Feel like?

WHY SHY PEOPLE
FEEL LIKE
DATING LOSERS

Loser. The word reeks of failure and self-loathing, of someone who has hit rock bottom and has nowhere to go. Unfortunately, a surprising number of shy people secretly think of themselves as dating losers, as hopeless outcasts who will never find their soul mates.

The problem lies in the way shy people interpret their romantic results. In a study I conducted a few years ago, I found that shy men tend to view their dating failures—when women turn them down for dates—as their fault. And they tend to see their dating successes as the results of outside factors, such as luck (she happened to be in a good mood when she agreed to go out). Non-shy men usually have the opposite view: They believe they succeed because of their own ability and effort, and if they fail, it's the result of bad luck (she was in a bad mood that day).

These results, which other researchers have duplicated with shy women, give further validity to the idea that shy people are mired in Observer-focused thinking. Shy people with strong Observers tend to think that every social encounter—every apparent acceptance or rejection—revolves around them and their social flaws.

Instead of recognizing that there are many reasons why someone may not respond well to them on a particular occasion (for example, the person may just have had a fight with a friend), shy people take the blame and believe others don't like them because they are flawed and damaged in some way.

To reverse this thinking, shy people need to develop a healthy Actor-Observer Balance. They need to see social situations more realistically and take more credit for their dating successes and less blame for their "dating failures." This change of perspective will in turn reinforce their self-esteem and encourage them to act in confident and positive ways that continue to bring them rewarding dating results.

STEP 2. Give your Observer a face. Draw the Observer using crayons, markers, or colored pencils, and include as much detail and as many colors as you want. Be creative. Draw the Observer's face or its whole body. Draw it sitting, standing still, or involved in an activity. You don't have to be a great artist to do this; just draw whatever comes to mind.

Another effective approach is to cut out a photograph (from a book, magazine, or newspaper) that reminds you of the Observer. Choose a picture that represents the Observer as a living, breathing creature that wants to do bad things to your social life.

STEP 3. As you look at your completed drawing or cutout picture, notice how you're feeling. Are you scared, angry, or depressed? Write down your feelings so you can be aware of just how much you've allowed the Observer to control your life until now.

Give the Observer a name that describes it and the havoc it has wreaked on your social life. Choose a name from TV, books, or movies, or make one up. Call it the Evil One, Genghis, Temptress, or anything else that seems to fit. Write the Observer's new name in large, bold letters at the top of the drawing or picture.

STEP 4. Duplicate the Observer's picture, and put up several copies around your house, perhaps in your bathroom, bedroom, or den. The more you're aware of the Observer, the less powerful it will seem, and the less influence it will have over you. You will see the Observer as a helpless entity that has influence only when it lives in the dark. When the Observer is exposed, it will evaporate like water in the sunlight.

Exercise 2. Separate Yourself from the Observer

In this follow-up exercise you will leave the Observer's image far behind as you make a bold declaration:

I AM NOT THE OBSERVER; THE OBSERVER IS NOT ME. MY TRUE IDENTITY IS SOMETHING PURE, BEAUTIFUL, AND NATURAL—SOMETHING FAR SUPERIOR TO THE PETTY, COWARDLY NATURE OF THE OBSERVER.

Here's what you do.

STEP 1. Place the Observer's picture in front of you as you sit in a chair or on the couch. Think of all the things the Observer has cost you: dates, friends, lovers, fun times, sex, peace of mind, self-confidence, marriage, family, children. Allow whatever feelings you have to bubble to the surface as you dig deep into your memory.

STEP 2. Stand up and look at the Observer, eye to eye. This is the moment you've been waiting for—your chance to tell the Observer exactly what you think of it. Begin with these words, saying them with as much power and conviction as you can muster: "You no longer control me, Observer. You are nothing but trash. I am free from your influence forever. I am free!"

STEP 3. Tell the Observer exactly how you feel in your own words. Get emotional, get intense. Let yourself go: Get angry, hostile, primitive. Jump up, scream, throw yourself on the floor (use a soft carpet to cushion your fall), tear up the Observer's picture if you want to. Release all those years of pent-up anger, disgust, and frustration; get everything the hell out.

STEP 4. Whenever you're in a social setting and you feel the Observer starting to rear its ugly head, begin a dialogue with yourself that challenges the Observer's presence. If you're feeling uneasy or uncomfortable at that big party, ask yourself: What is the Observer saying to me right now? Do I really believe what it's telling me? If you find yourself avoiding that attractive person you're dying to meet, ask yourself: Why am I shying away like this? How is the Observer involved here?

If you commit to this exercise you will experience an incredible sense of relief and empowerment. For perhaps the first time in your life, you will stand up to the Observer and declare your social freedom. You will mark this moment forever as your day of social independence, the day you revolted against the Observer and elevated yourself to your rightful place: the master of your social destiny.

Dancing with the Actor

Ever since her husband died three years ago, fifty-five-year-old Bernadette—a shy attractive silver-haired schoolteacher—felt lost and lonely. Walter, her extremely outgoing, Extraverted husband, had been not only her loving partner for twenty-seven years but also her guiding light in social situations. Whenever they were at a party, Bernadette had the luxury of falling back into her shy, quiet self while Walter mingled and networked. Walter had a knack for introducing new people to Bernadette and keeping the conversation alive. All Bernadette had to do was relax and listen as her social maestro lit up the room with style and charisma.

Now that Walter was gone and she was single again, Bernadette was struggling to find her own social identity. Not only was she as shy as ever but she was also thirty years out of practice when it came to dating.

When Bernadette came to me for shyness coaching, she was very depressed. She spent almost all of her leisure time at home reading self-help books, and she had few friends and social outlets. Because of her intense shyness, she seriously doubted whether she would ever start dating again and find a man as marvelous as her Walter.

I suggested that Bernadette become best friends with her Actor—the fun-loving and spontaneous part of her personality. I asked her: "Can you think of a time when your Actor was in charge and you felt really attractive and desirable?"

"Yes," she replied. "Early in our marriage, we went on a cruise to Cancún. There was one special night, our last, when I was all dressed up in a beautiful red dress, and I felt special and sexy, just like a movie star."

With this memory to guide her, Bernadette drew several color pictures of her outgoing, charismatic Actor—which she called the Lady in Red—and put them up all over her house. Whenever Bernadette felt anxious about going to a social event, she meditated on the pictures of her true self, the Lady in Red, and instantly she would feel more relaxed, attractive, and confident.

Slowly Bernadette built up her confidence and began dating. One night she called me: "Dr. Avila, I've met a fantastic man. He's sixty-two, a retired pharmacist; smart, outgoing, and stocky, just the way I like 'em. We really hit it off, and we're going steady now. And guess what, Dr. Avila?"

"What?" I asked.

"The first night we went out I put on a pretty red dress, and I was her—the Lady in Red. I felt so confident and relaxed; it was just like that time on the cruise.

"I'm still shy, but I'm not afraid now because I know the Lady in Red will be there for me, just like Walter was. I'm not alone anymore."

Deep in the soul of every shy person there dwells a playful child, a delightfully cute creature who plays, prances, laughs, and sings—unbothered by the stiffness and stuffiness of the adult social world. Dancing. Getting crazy. Throwing mud pies. Making funny faces. Telling silly jokes. This spunky little creature is, of course, the Actor: that wonderfully spontaneous and creative part of your mind that just wants to have fun.

It's too bad many shy people have misplaced their Actor. They forgot (or maybe never learned) what it's like to have fun. They take their social lives way too seriously, are constantly worried about looking foolish or inadequate, and are overly preoccupied with how others are perceiving them. In time anxiety, rigidity, and futility set in, and shy people lose the enthusiasm and playfulness they had as children. They lack that lightness-of-being a person has when he or she no longer cares about trying to impress others and instead focuses on just having fun.

It all boils down to one word: *spontaneity*. Spontaneity is the fuel of the Actor, the engine that jump-starts conversations, provides social flow, and keeps relationships bubbling with excitement. To be spontaneous means you're open and receptive to life, you participate in life through being instead of thinking, and you're always on the lookout for the novel, the fresh, and the unexpected.

When you're spontaneous you're also able to

- *Think quickly on your feet.* You're not hampered by the Observer's "Let's keep analyzing this so we don't screw it up" commentary that freezes your mind and prevents you from acting spontaneously. You are, instead, able to act and speak freely from your gut in a smooth and effortless manner that helps you get what you want from any social encounter.
- *Take intelligent social risks.* You are not afraid to take risks because you know the only real risk is the one not taken. Spontaneity urges you to action; anything less would feel uncomfortable because you wouldn't be expressing the real you.
- *Leave yourself a large margin for error in social settings.* You tell yourself: "I may make social mistakes in the future, but I will not let them stop me from being carefree and spontaneous." With this carefree mind-set, you will no longer be frozen in intimidating social situations. You will know that, even if you make a mistake, you will learn something valuable from the experience, and you will move one step closer to achieving your romantic goals.
- *Experiment with new behaviors and alternate responses.* You're not tied to the same old opening lines ("What do you do for a living?") or stale dating strategies (singles dances every second Saturday). Now you're free to explore new conversational strategies, people, and activities because you crave the creativity, novelty, and pleasure of stepping out of the ordinary and trying something different.

When you're fully spontaneous and in your Actor mode, you can converse fluidly and naturally, offer or accept an invitation smoothly, and exit gracefully when the time is right. You're in full social command, no matter who you're talking to, no matter what the environment.

As you develop your spontaneous Actor, realize this: Being spontaneous doesn't mean you have to be loud, arrogant, or a showboat. It doesn't mean you have to be a flaming party animal who doesn't know when to stop. Spontaneous shy people can still be quiet, unassuming, and sensitive. Their spontaneity comes from their ability to be 100 percent authentic, free-flowing, and present in everything they do, whether they're talking, dancing, or singing in the shower.

ImprovTherapy: How to Be a Star
in Your Own Romantic Show

Imagine you could be the star of your own romantic movie: You could write the perfect love story, choose your ideal leading man or lady, and live happily ever after. Now there is a way for you to plot your social life and create a happy romantic ending for yourself through the power of ImprovTherapy.

ImprovTherapy is a shy-friendly approach that combines psychodrama (a form of therapy that uses role playing) and improvisational acting (theater games that actors use to improve their spontaneity and acting skills) to help you become a more spontaneous, free-flowing, and socially confident person. ImprovTherapy works by taking the pressure off your social performance. Rather than taking your dating life too seriously, you see yourself as an actor in a fun and ever-changing social play.

As you learn the ImprovTherapy approach, your entire attitude toward dating will change: Whereas before, you may have approached dating with an anxious and intense attitude, now you will see yourself as a relaxed and confident Actor in a living social theater. You will talk spontaneously and naturally to everyone you meet—not just to get a date or meet your soul mate but to improve your acting skills and fully express your Actor's nature in a fun, genuine, and creative way.

With this new approach you can enjoy trying out different dating characters just like you would try on funny hats in front of a mirror. You can, for example, play the shy flirt, the flamboyant party animal, the cool intellectual type. Because you're only acting, you won't take it so personally if someone doesn't like one of your characters. He or she is not rejecting you, just one of the roles you have decided to play, one of the hats you have decided to wear. It's no big deal.

Of course, some people immediately ask: "Aren't you being phony when you pretend to be someone you're not? If you're acting, you're not being yourself; you're being fake."

On the contrary. The more of an Actor you become, the more authentic and natural you will be. The Actor is the true one; the Ob-

THE BIRTH OF IMPROVTHERAPY

Aristotle believed that drama could be used to provoke a catharsis—a powerful release of emotions that would purge a person's soul and bring about healing. When watching the beautiful and tragic plays of ancient Greece, members of the audience could experience this catharsis by identifying with the characters and seeing parallels in their own lives.

In the early twentieth century the Viennese psychiatrist Jacob Levy Moreno developed psychodrama—the use of drama as a form of group therapy—to help patients work through crises and conflicts. Moreno believed psychologically disturbed patients could gain emotional release and insight if they were given the freedom to re-create emotional scenes from their past.

In the 1990s I developed a new program, ImprovTherapy, to help shy people achieve social mastery based on the principles of psychodrama and improvisational acting. It all started in 1985, when I took an improvisational acting class for fun and discovered an unexpected side effect: After the class my social confidence soared, and I was more successful at meeting appealing women than ever before.

By applying improvisational acting techniques to my personal life, I could access sweet parts of myself—bold, funny, and flirtatious—that had been hidden deep within my shyness. Not only was this fun and liberating but it also gave me an incredible realization:

> If I could teach shy people how to access the power of their Actor, they, too, could transform their shyness into a dating advantage and find their soul mates.

Later I saw the tremendous progress my students made as they applied the ImprovTherapy techniques I taught them. In a short time many of my students—including those who had dated very little and were desperately lonely—were able to significantly improve the quantity and quality of their dates, en route to developing lasting relationships.

server is the fake. For years the Observer has placed a self-conscious shy mask over your face to prevent you from displaying the true parts of you. All those roles and characters you play as a social Actor—sexy, confident, flirtatious, and so forth—have always been small parts of the real you. They were just buried under the Observer's facade until your Actor could rescue them.

You're already an actor—someone who plays different roles depending on the situation. In a typical day you may play parent, student, worker, friend, sibling, citizen, and, of course, your Academy Award–winning favorite—the self-conscious shy person. The difference with ImprovTherapy is that you will become a *conscious* Actor in your social life. Rather than playing just one fixed role— the self-conscious shy person—you will choose the roles you want to play. You may be a shy maiden one moment, a dating diva the next. With gusto and creativity you will explore your hidden social talents and have fun with all the intriguing parts of your personality.

As you play these different roles, you will experiment with the Actor's tools—the different parts of mind and body that actors use to create a vivid and realistic experience for their audiences. You can, for example, vary vocal quality, nonverbal expressions, conversational approaches, and the like, depending on your goals in a social situation. Unlike that of a professional actor, however, your goal is not to entertain or enlighten but to work on yourself—to develop inner mastery and social confidence, regardless of how initially successful you are with potential romantic partners.

That last point is key. If you can become completely committed to developing your Actor, regardless of any possible romantic outcomes, you will be liberated from the agony of unfulfilled expectations, never-ending regret, and paralyzing self-consciousness. You will be free to explore your social-romantic potential in a way that will bring you more fun, pleasure, and success than you ever imagined possible.

When you see romantic encounters as merely fun acting exercises, a miraculous transformation will occur: You will stop taking yourself so seriously, and you will finally begin to enjoy yourself in the dating world. You will still take the prospect of finding a soul mate seriously; you will still display absolute respect for your dating partners. The big difference will be that you no longer feel pressured to excel; you can simply relax and let success come to you naturally, without stress and strain.

ImprovTherapy Exercises for Your Actor

In the following exercises you will learn how to use the Actor's tools to become socially confident and romantically successful. You will be the type of person who can create dating magic wherever you go.

Exercise 1. Give Your Actor a Face

It's time to invite your Actor up onstage by giving it a face. Unlike the Observer, who becomes weaker when it's exposed, the Actor becomes stronger.

STEP 1. Recall a time when the Actor was front and center in your social life; when you felt charming, attractive, and irresistible. Maybe it was that wild night out with your friends, that once-in-a-lifetime birthday party, or that special date with your dream person. On that unforgettable occasion, you were in heaven: You had such an incredibly fun time, and everything you did worked out beautifully as you oozed sexual and romantic appeal.

If you can't recall such a time—or never had one—think of someone you know, or even a character from TV, movies, or books, who embodies the confidence, grace, and charisma of the Actor. Imagine you're that person. See yourself as the type of person who knows exactly what to do in any social situation and always ends up having more fun than anyone else.

STEP 2. Meditate on your Actor, and experience it as completely as you can through your five senses. See, taste, feel, touch, and hear your Actor.

STEP 3. Using your favorite drawing tools, draw the Actor in as much detail and color as you can. Don't worry about being a great artist; just do the best you can. Your goal here is to capture the simple essence of your Actor as you experience it in the present moment.

If drawing isn't your thing, cut out a picture that captures the essence of your Actor from a magazine, newspaper, or book. Find a picture that symbolizes the light spirit of your Actor: its fun, playfulness, and unparalleled spontaneity.

STEP 4. Look at your drawing or picture, and become aware of any feelings you're experiencing, including lightness, joy, and sexiness. Bask in the warm feelings your hero or heroine, the Actor, brings to your heart. Give your Actor a name—Light Goddess, Delilah, Bambi, Showman, Hercules—anything you can think of. Choose a name from books, movies, or history, or think up one on your own. Make sure the name you choose captures the charming and beautiful essence of the Actor. Write the Actor's full name in bold letters at the top of your drawing.

STEP 5. Make copies of your Actor's image, and put them up everywhere you can think of, including your car dashboard, kitchen, bedroom, or bathroom. To emphasize the Actor's power, you can place its picture next to the Observer's. Eventually you may want to put the Actor's image over the Observer's, covering it up completely as you symbolically (and in reality) put the dynamic Actor first in your social life.

As you make the Actor's face a big part of your daily life, you will experience a growing sense of social confidence, and you will be one step closer to finding your soul mate.

Exercise 2. Make Your Actor Come Alive

Champagne was pouring, music was rocking, and twenty-nine-year-old Jackie was having the time of her life at her friend's wedding reception. All the handsome guys she could imagine were there, and she was eager to meet the best of the best. Everything was going beautifully until she laid eyes on Alex, an impossibly handsome twenty-seven-year-old concert promoter with long wavy black hair, incredible eyes, and a body to die for. Not only was Alex sexy and successful but he was also a caring family man: Since his aunt's stroke, he had paid her medical bills and had given up work to care for her. He was a real gem.

"There's no way you'll ever get a man like that," said Jackie's Observer. "No way. He's just too good for you. Forget it." With these thoughts ricocheting in her mind like pinballs, Jackie suddenly felt very depressed. The memories flooded in: She was in high school again and dreamed about Troy, Mr. Everything—star athlete, model, and class president. She wanted him so bad, but in four years the closest she ever got to Troy was asking him to donate some money for the science club fund-raiser.

Stop it, Jackie told herself, as she interrupted her memory train back to high school. Quickly she went to the bathroom and started posing in front of the mirror as Delilah, that irresistible queen of womanhood who could have any man she desired. Her posture, facial expression, and mood were transformed. She was sultry, seductive, and powerful. She *was* Delilah.

Now poised, Jackie strode up to Alex and said: "Hi there. I don't believe we've met."

"No, we haven't," replied Alex, impressed by Jackie's directness. "I'm Alex."

"I'm Jackie."

With these simple words Jackie and Alex entered into a fascinating conversation that ended up at Alex's place for an incredible night of passionate lovemaking and cuddling by the fireplace. Jackie had never felt so wonderful with a man, and she knew, deep down, that he was the One.

Although the Actor inside you is not always easy to find, its fun, laughter, and brilliance make the effort well worth it. Once you let your Actor come out to play, your social life will never be the same again. Let's energize your Actor now.

STEP 1. Take your Actor's picture and place it in front of you. Remember all the fun social experiences the Actor has provided for you in the past. Envision all the pleasures the Actor has in store for you in the future.

STEP 2. Immediately go to your kitchen, closet, garage, or storage room, and pick out the things your Actor would enjoy. Choose Actor-friendly cologne, perfume, or makeup. Find that funny hat, colorful scarf, or wild tie you rarely wear. Pick up the book, magazine, or video that has "Actor" written all over it. Whatever you do, don't censor your thoughts; simply let the Actor come out of you, choosing what it wants. When the Actor wants something, you'll know it.

STEP 3. Experience whatever your Actor has picked out for you. Don't think about it; just do it. Twirl that baton, put on those sunglasses, don that Mexican hat. Watch that trashy fun video. Make yourself a tangy and spicy snack, put on some sexy music, and let the party begin! Look at yourself in the mirror as the Actor exudes irrepressible joy, spontaneity, and sexiness. Cap it all off with your Actor's sexy, resonant voice saying whatever comes to mind: "I'm sexy, irresistible, and a wonder to behold. Watch out, world; here I come!"

STEP 4. Whenever you're in an intimidating social situation, excuse yourself for a moment—go to a bathroom or private place—and meditate on your Actor. Think of all the things the Actor loves, its favorite clothes, scents, music, movies, foods, activities, and jokes. Visualize your Actor rising inside you—taking over your body, emotions, and soul.

As you meditate on your Actor, you will experience a remarkable transformation: Your posture will straighten, your breathing will deepen, your voice will resonate with a musical quality, and your mood and confidence will soar. Soon you will be ready to reenter the party as a totally new person: the Actor.

Between the Actor and the Observer:
The Perfect Social Balance

Now that your Actor is jammin' and jivin', you may start to believe that the Actor is all you need. If that's the case, you have to slow down for a moment and realize this: To be socially successful, you need to be the Actor, but you also need to have *some* of the Observer.

The Observer offers an interesting paradox: It can, at times, actually help you improve your social life. Although much of what your parents, peers, and others told you about your social skills and outlook may have been inaccurate and unhelpful, some of what they said had some merit. Maybe you *did* need to speak more clearly, look people in the eye more, and maintain straighter posture.

It's true that we can sometimes learn from those who criticize us, regardless of their motives, because they see us from a perspective outside our own self-interest. The key, of course, is to ignore what is mean-spirited or just plain wrong and digest the few kernels of truth in their critiques.

Not only can the Observer give you valuable social feedback from time to time but, in small doses, it can also serve as your conscience. Like Freud's superego, the Observer can keep you in line when you're tempted to do something that's harmful, inappropriate, or just plain dumb. If you get the sudden urge to indulge in a tasteless joke, drink too much, or make an unwanted pass at someone, the Observer will smack you upside the head and yell: "Stop! Don't make an ass out of yourself!"

Used rightly, the Observer can be like a good old-fashioned parent who lays down the laws of polite society and expects you to comply. The rules are not just for form's sake but are intended to keep you out of trouble so you can enjoy a happy and productive life.

Psychologists have found that socially successful people have approximately 70 to 80 percent of the Actor and 20 to 30 percent of the Observer in their personalities. Shy people, and others who suffer from self-conscious maladies such as stuttering, tend to have too much Observer (90 percent or more) and not enough Actor (10 percent or less). These overly self-conscious people spend most of their time second-guessing themselves and not enough time acting spontaneously and naturally. By contrast, people who are sociopaths—those who act irresponsibly and without guilt—tend to have too much of the Actor (90 percent or more) and not enough of the conscientious Observer (only 10 percent or less). These greedy, selfish, and irresponsible people rarely think about their actions; they simply do what they want to do, and to hell with the consequences.

If you want to be a socially successful person, you need to develop that ideal balance of approximately 70 to 80 percent Actor and 20 to 30 percent Observer. With this just-right blend you will have enough Observer to provide you with a social conscience, and enough Actor to keep you acting freely, without excessive self-consciousness.

Take the Actor-Observer Quiz

To determine your current level of Actor and Observer, take the following quiz. Circle the number that corresponds with how much you agree or disagree with each of the statements, ranging from 1 (strongly disagree) to 10 (strongly agree). If you circle 5, that means you're neutral on the statement.

1. I don't always say whatever comes to mind when I'm in the presence of strangers.
   1   2   3   4   5   6   7   8   9   10

2. I don't usually act in outrageously silly ways—dancing on tables, and so forth—when I'm at parties and social events.
   1   2   3   4   5   6   7   8   9   10

3. I'm not the kind of person who easily approaches attractive strangers and asks them out on dates.
   1   2   3   4   5   6   7   8   9   10

4. I'm not the type of person who takes a lot of risks in social-romantic situations.
   1   2   3   4   5   6   7   8   9   10

5. I'm not known as a huge party animal.
   1   2   3   4   5   6   7   8   9   10

6. I sometimes feel self-conscious when I'm with attractive and interesting people.
   1   2   3   4   5   6   7   8   9   10

7. I remember a time (or several times) when I was interested in someone but didn't do anything because I was afraid of what others would think.
   1   2   3   4   5   6   7   8   9   10

8. When I'm around a person I'm really attracted to, I may excessively think about, and mentally rehearse, what I'm going to say because I don't want to say the wrong thing.
   1   2   3   4   5   6   7   8   9   10

9. If I'm at an important party or social event, I sometimes feel that people are judging me.
   1   2   3   4   5   6   7   8   9   10

10. When I'm not able to connect with the desirable person I wanted to meet, I may feel some regret.
    1   2   3   4   5   6   7   8   9   10

Scoring

Add up your points. This number is your Observer score. Then subtract that number from 100; the remaining figure is your Actor score. If, for example, you scored 80, your Observer score is 80, and your Actor score is 20 (100 – 80).

Put your scores here:

Actor Score ____
Observer Score ____

Now check out your profile:

Observer 70–100, Actor 30–0: You have a very strong Observer, which makes you feel self-conscious, embarrassed, and regretful in social encounters. The Observer is always putting your social performance under strict scrutiny. You will benefit by carefully studying the next four chapters and learning how to develop more of your Actor and less of your Observer.

Observer 50–69, Actor 31–50: You have a strong Observer and a relatively weak Actor. You can profit from the material in the next four chapters as you focus on strengthening your Actor.

Observer 31–49, Actor 51–69: You have a moderately strong Actor and a relatively weak Observer. Although you're on the right track, you still need to do some work to increase your spontaneity.

Observer 20–30, Actor 70–80: This is what you should strive for: the ideal balance between the Actor and the Observer. With this combination you will be free-flowing and unself-conscious, yet mature and self-aware.

Observer 0–19, Actor 81–100: This combination can cause some problems, especially if you're at the higher end of the Actor (if your Actor is 90 or greater). With a very high Actor score, a person may act foolishly and even harmfully toward others, without paying much attention to the consequences. If you're shy, you probably won't score this high on the Actor, but if you do, you need to tone it down a bit.

CHAPTER 6

Warming Up

The more Kristie, a shy divorced thirty-seven-year-old actress, thought about going to the party, the less she liked the idea. There would be handsome men there, of course; her friend Cher had a knack for handpicking the best-looking single men for her parties. But that was exactly the problem. Kristie would have to face them without knowing what to say. She would get hypernervous, she would blush, and by the end of the night she would be totally embarrassed.

To make matters worse, Cher would launch into her matchmaker spiel, telling any man within shouting distance about Kristie's accomplishments as an actress and her merits as a potential wife. Cher was happily married and loved to play matchmaker for her single friends, but Kristie hated the whole idea. She almost felt like throwing up when she imagined what Cher would say this time: "Kristie here has been in tons of commercials and soap operas. She's a great actress, beautiful and, of course, a great cook. You know, she really loves children. Why don't you two get better acquainted?"

Yikes. Now Cher was due any minute, and the whole nightmare was about to start all over again. Quickly, Kristie tried to think of a believable excuse she could use for avoiding the party.

Grandma in town? No, she used that one last time. Brother in jail? No, her brother was a saint. Tabitha, her cat, hit by a car? Yes, that would work. But it was such a horrible lie. She would definitely have to make it up to Tabitha later by spoiling her with her favorite salmon sushi.

Kristie hated to lie, but she had to get out of the party or she was definitely going to regret it.

How many times have you wished you could get out of a social engagement because you felt too anxious or insecure to face the people you were going to meet? How often have you decided you just weren't ready to face that attractive person who could be *the* one? For many shy people the word *pressure* immediately comes to mind when they think of coming into contact with—and being judged and possibly rejected by—attractive and desirable people.

Because you're a shy person, your biggest dating challenge often comes at the beginning—when you first think about going out and meeting sexy strangers. That's when you're clobbered by all those Observer-manufactured thoughts: "You don't belong there. You'll make a fool out of yourself. That gorgeous person will never be interested in someone (insert here: ugly, old, shy, boring . . .) like you." As the Observer reigns over your thoughts, your blood pressure increases, your pulse accelerates, and your anxiety becomes an uncontrollable force of nature.

Although your social stage fright can seem overwhelming at times, there *is* good news: You have, right in the palm of your hand, a perfect antidote to your dating jitters. I'm talking about the Actor's favorite friend, the warm-up: the step-by-step process of gradually increasing your comfort level until you're ready to face the world.

The truth is that shy people often need a considerable warm-up period before they can feel comfortable and relaxed in a social environment. Because shy people tend to have delicate nervous systems, they can be easily overwhelmed by crowds, loud noises, smoke, and the like. They need time to get their nervous systems accustomed to potentially stressful environments. Shy people also tend to be very socially sensitive—they're especially vulnerable to perceived slights and rejections, and they can react badly if they think others don't like them. If shy people don't feel liked and accepted when they first enter a social situation, they may withdraw to protect themselves from being rejected, embarrassed, and humiliated.

It's no wonder, then, that shy people need a longer than average warm-up period to feel comfortable in social situations. They have much more to work through—more emotions to deal with, more anxieties and insecurities to overcome. Shy people need that extra time to soothe their social jitters, toughen their psychological skin, and prepare themselves for the dating wars.

Melting Social Tension Like Butter

"She's a knockout and really nice, too. Don't worry, you'll have a great time." Those were the soothing words from Oleg's cousin Vasily as he described Tatiana, Oleg's blind date for the evening. Oleg, a thirty-four-year-old electrical engineer, had recently broken up with his girlfriend of seven years and was cautiously testing the dating waters. Because Oleg was shy, he found it difficult to meet new women; he had always relied on friends and family to introduce him to eligible ladies. Although his cousin was reassuring, Oleg still felt nervous—after all, he had been out of the dating market for a long time, and he didn't know what to expect.

Fortunately, Vasily was a dating expert, and he was able to guide Oleg through a series of warm-up exercises to help him feel confident and relaxed. Although skeptical at first, Oleg found that exercises worked really well. By the time he was ready to meet Tatiana, he was feeling much more relaxed and comfortable.

Oleg made a good impression on Tatiana and ended up having a great time with her. He even surprised himself by giving her a long, lingering kiss at the end of the night without his usual awkwardness. And, best of all, Oleg discovered that Vasily had been right: Tatiana was really a nice and attractive lady, and they ended up liking each other a lot.

At this point in his life, Oleg is not certain if he's ready for another long-term relationship, but he's having a fantastic time dating Tatiana, and he's sure glad he listened to his cousin.

When shy people are tense and anxious in social situations, their muscles become stiff, their speech becomes fast and forced (or the opposite: slow and nonexistent), and their thinking becomes inflexible, hackneyed, and humorless. Because most of this tension occurs even before you're in a social interaction, I call it *presocial tension*: the physical and emotional stress you experience when you worry about all the bad things that can happen to you in a social situation. You're already cringing at the no you're expecting from that alluring person you've been obsessing about for the past four weeks. You're already stressing about the large dinner party you've been invited to, an intimidating place filled with people who seem way out of your league.

Even though tension generally has a negative impact on your social life, there is one area where it can have a positive benefit: When you're interacting with a potential romantic candidate, your tension is the signal that you're talking to the right person. You will feel the most anxiety when the stakes are the highest; when you're with someone you're really attracted to. By contrast, when you're with someone you don't find very desirable, it's easy to be calm and relaxed because there's nothing at stake; there's nothing to lose.

If you see your tension as a normal part of romantic attraction, you won't be so intimidated by the feelings you're experiencing. You will realize that your feelings are the signal you're on the right track; you're with the person who could end up being your soul mate.

Although it's not always easy to rise above those feelings of anxiety and dread when you're with a desirable person, it can be done. To develop this type of self-mastery, it's a good idea to practice the relaxation response—the way to fully relax your mind and body.

Exercise 1. The Relaxation Response

Before you go out for the evening, take the following steps.

STEP 1. Lie on the floor, face up, with your eyes closed. Imagine that the floor beneath you has become an endlessly deep marshmallow pit. See yourself sinking into this pit, deeper and deeper, as the pleasantly gooey, soft, and warm marshmallows absorb all your stress and leave you feeling cozy and relaxed.

STEP 2. Notice how relaxed and loose your body and mind are becoming. Let yourself go, and feel the all-embracing peace, tranquillity, and safety of this marshmallow sanctuary.

STEP 3. Imagine that this marshmallow pit has wrapped itself around you as a protective covering that is with you wherever you go. No matter what situation you're in, you will feel the warmth and relaxation of this cocoon as it shields you from the stresses and strains of the social world.

Finding the Center

Whenever Tammy, a thirty-nine-year-old investment banker, walked into a room, something exciting usually happened. Men would swivel their heads and feel her enchanting energy. Some would experience such a strong pulse of excitement and attraction that they would interrupt their conversations and scurry over to Tammy like puppets on strings.

The mysterious attraction men felt toward Tammy wasn't about her looks; actually she was quite average, with silver streaks in her hair, plain features, and a plump body. She dressed well, but there was definitely something else about Tammy that made her so irresistible. Tammy's secret was simple: She knew how to tap into the energy center of her body. With her powerful energy radiating out, she attracted interesting men from all walks of life. They approached her in bookstores, grocery stores, coffee shops—anywhere she went.

Although it was scary, exciting, and overwhelming at times, Tammy soon learned how to project her energy outward in the right situations and toward those men she really wanted to meet. It had worked beautifully, and now Tammy was happily dating three great men: one from the entertainment business, another from politics, and the third a self-made millionaire in the computer industry. All three were charming, attractive, and successful, and Tammy had a tough time choosing the best. It was a nice problem to have, and she was going to take her time figuring it out.

There is something powerful in your stomach—a special point approximately two inches below your navel that martial artists and Eastern philosophers call the Tan Tien (pronounced "Dahn T-yen"). This point is located in the center of your body and serves as the storage place for all your psychological and emotional energy. When martial artists want to display the utmost physical power, they concentrate all their attention on breathing, moving, and acting from their Tan Tien.

For shy people the Tan Tien is their gut instinct, their Actor. When they think and act from this powerful energy point, they're spontaneous, free-flowing, and self-confident. They know exactly what to say and do because the truth flows naturally from their gut. The Tan Tien state of mind is the exact opposite of the Observer mind-set. When you're focused on your Tan Tien, you don't have to analyze, and struggle with, what you want to say in a social situation. The words flow to you automatically; you actually feel the words, thoughts, and feelings being lifted from the pit of your stomach.

Although the Tan Tien can offer you so much, it may not come naturally to you at first. When you begin to focus on this energy point, you may feel some uneasiness and tension. You might even feel a bit foolish. You may think: Come on; I'm supposed to think and act from my stomach? What kind of crazy fool thing is that?

Before you go any further, take a step back and see what's really going on. If you listen closely to the critical voice in your head, you will detect the unmistakable rasping of your old nemesis—the Observer. The Observer hates your Tan Tien and will do anything it can to keep you away from it. Your Observer wants to keep you mired in the confusion of overanalysis, self-judgment, doubts, and worries. It doesn't want you to experience the fresh air of unfettered spontaneity and maximum mental flexibility that comes from your gut.

Every time you're being overly analytical, you can bet the Observer is trying to exert its influence. If you stutter, stumble, mumble, blank out, drop something, or simply walk away fearfully during a social encounter, you can bet the Observer is at it again. Whenever you feel the Observer trying to take over, direct your focus back to your Tan Tien. See your entire point of focus, your very essence, coming from that special point as you fully experience the stability and power that flow smoothly from your natural energy center.

Think back to your childhood for a moment. If you were like most children, you probably played spontaneously and acted from your gut instinct. Unfortunately, your parents, peers, and society soon stepped in and told you it wasn't good or proper to be so loud, playful, and spontaneous. Before long, you lost your urge to be natural and free, and your Tan Tien–focused life was gradually replaced by an Observer-dominated existence. You moved from your gut to your head, from a natural, balanced nature to a reflective existence that made you second-guess your every move.

Exercise 2. Tan Tien Versus Head

To experience the difference between living from your Tan Tien and living from your head, get one of your friends to help you in this exercise.

STEP 1. Stand with your feet shoulder width apart and your arms at your sides. Concentrate all your attention on the tip of your head; see your whole being as it emanates from that spot. Your entire point of concentration, your psychological focus, is 100 percent on the tip of your head: Your eyes are there, your mind, your hands, everything.

Now ask your friend to apply slow, steady, and firm pressure to your chest with his or her fingertips, pushing you as far back as possible. Don't try to resist; simply let your body respond to the pressure. See how far you're pushed back.

STEP 2. Without changing your stance, switch your point of concentration from your head to your Tan Tien, two inches below your navel. See your entire being emanating from this point—your eyes, mind, and breath—as you slowly inhale through your nose and exhale from your mouth. Visualize the powerful energy of the Tan Tien as it travels on the wings of your breath throughout your body, revitalizing you and giving you power and confidence.

Ask your friend to apply the same amount of fingertip pressure as before. Again, don't resist as your friend pushes you back. Simply let your body move in response to the pressure.

Notice the difference between Steps 1 and 2. Chances are, your friend was able to push you far more easily and much farther back when your point of concentration was on the tip of your head than when you were centered in your Tan Tien. Determine this for yourself.

STEP 3. Repeat Steps 1 and 2, except this time have your friend assume the stance, and you do the pushing. Notice how far you are able to push your friend as you apply the same pressure each time.

If you do this exercise properly, you will be surprised at how easily you can be pushed off balance when you think from your head (the Observer) and how firm and stable you are when you think from your Tan Tien (your Actor).

In social situations shy people tend to lead with their heads, always analyzing and worrying about the outcome—always off balance, nervously awaiting the first psychological push, the first rejection, which will send them crashing to the floor. When you lead with your gut, by contrast, the results will be far superior. Your voice will be deeper and more resonant, your posture will be straighter, and your muscles will be more relaxed. Overall, you will be much more spontaneous, confident, and attractive than ever before.

Exercise 3. Expanding Your Tan Tien

When you focus on your Tan Tien on a daily basis, you'll find that others will be attracted to your irresistible energy. People you don't know may smile at you for no reason, come over and talk with you, and pay you compliments. It's all because your energy is so vital, so alive, and so attractive that others will want to get close to you and savor its power. To harness your Tan Tien as a powerful tool for romantic attraction, do this exercise before you go to a social event.

STEP 1. Go to your favorite room and stand with your feet shoulder width apart and your arms at your sides. Take a deep breath and imagine that your Tan Tien is a powerful spotlight that shines a beautiful light all over the room. Think of the spotlight's color; perhaps it's blood red, hot pink, or crystal white. Visualize this colored light filling up the room with a warm, beautiful, and joyous feeling. As the loving energy circulates through the room, feel yourself becoming more confident, lovable, and joyous.

STEP 2. When you enter a social situation, go to the bathroom or a private place to warm up your Tan Tien. Stand normally with your eyes open, take a deep breath—inhaling through your nose—and imagine that your breath is carrying the colored light of the Tan Tien. Visualize this colored breath as it travels up your nostrils, down the back of your head, spine, buttocks, legs, and up from your feet; through your legs, stomach, chest, and out through your mouth. As this breath travels throughout your body, feel its calming and energizing effect, a rush of vitality and well-being.

STEP 3. Walk into the main area of the social setting and stand still for a moment. In your mind's eye see the special colored light as it sprays out from your Tan Tien and pinpoints those interesting and attractive people you would like to meet. Try not to add any expectations to your energy; don't expect any particular person to recognize and respond to it. Your only goal is to express and shine your energy outward because it feels good and natural to do so. If someone responds favorably (as a few select individuals will), that's simply an added bonus.

With your Tan Tien guiding you, you will not only shine outwardly as a sexy and attractive person, but you will also shine inwardly. You will feel much better about yourself, and you will carry yourself in a confident and powerful manner.

The First One Doesn't Count

Felix, a shy, thirty-six-year-old CPA, had an all-or-nothing attitude toward women. Either a woman had the full package—beauty, brains, and personality—or he didn't want to put out the energy to try to meet her. The problem was that Felix rarely met a woman who reached his high standards, and even when he did he was too shy to do anything about it. On the few occasions when he was face-to-face with his ideal woman, Felix would freeze up and blow his opportunity to get to know her better. Then he would feel regretful and attack himself for his stupidity and ineptness.

When Felix began shyness coaching, he realized how he had been sabotaging himself, and he decided to try a new approach: Rather than spend all night scoping out the best-looking women, Felix would move into action as soon as he arrived. First, he would spot a plain-looking woman who was sitting by herself and looking bored and lonely. Summoning up all his courage and charm, he would smile, approach her, and ask her to dance.

Most of the time the lonely lady would say yes, and Felix would have instant success. He would dance with her and feel a positive vibe from his grateful dance partner. From there he would keep interacting with other women who weren't exactly his type but who were kind and receptive to him. By the end of the night Felix would be such a ball of charm and energy that even some of the most attractive and desirable women at the dance would want to know him better.

At his last singles dance he met Samantha, a tall, voluptuous thirty-three-year-old singer who reminded him of an angel in the desert. Surrounded by ravenous men all night, Samantha made it a point to approach Felix and compliment him on his dancing. She was impressed with his energy and style, and the fact that he was dancing with everyone: young, old, fat, skinny, plain, attractive. He came across as a nice guy who was open to people and wasn't just interested in one thing.

Felix found Samantha a classy lady in her own right, and he was thrilled when she accepted his invitation to go out dancing. They've been together for three months now, and Felix knows he has found his dream woman—the full package.

If you're shy, here's a secret: You don't have to hit the romantic jackpot on the first pull; you don't have to interact with the most attractive person in the room when you first walk in.

Many shy people feel a tremendous amount of pressure in social situations because they suffer from what's known as the approach-avoidance conflict. On the one hand, they want to approach an attractive person and perhaps develop an intimate connection with him or her. On the other hand, they're petrified of being rejected or embarrassed, so they often end up avoiding that dazzling person altogether. Torn by these equally powerful urges, shy people often end up frustrated and defeated because they don't know which way to turn.

The solution is to neither advance nor retreat but to gradually enter the dating fray and notch some easy victories. Start by having simple conversations with people who may not be your type but who will provide you with a measure of confidence and social flow. Then, when you're sufficiently warmed up, you can talk with the gorgeous person you're *really* interested in.

When you warm up like this, you get a feel for what it's like to have successful conversations with several nonthreatening people first—the bartender, a business acquaintance, an average-looking person who's not your type—before you converse with that really attractive person you've been pining over. You can use each small conversational success as a minor painkiller that alleviates your anxiety and propels you toward meeting increasingly attractive and desirable people.

This approach not only increases your self-confidence and comfort level but also changes the way you look at social interactions. Rather than seeing every encounter as a crucial judgment of your social competence, you see each one as just another stepping-stone toward honing your skills and eventually meeting the person you really want to meet.

As a shy person, you tend to turn each social interaction into an all-or-nothing, do-or-die scenario that reflects (usually badly) on your social skills and self-worth. When you're face-to-face with an attractive person, you might think thoughts like these: "He looked away for a moment; he hates the way I look." "She didn't laugh at my joke; she thinks I'm stupid."

With the "first one doesn't count" approach, you will no longer be so harsh on yourself. Rather than scrutinizing all your interactions under a microscope as absolute measures of your social worth, you will see them as fun and convenient ways to warm up your Actor's muscles, much as an opera singer sings scales to warm up his or her vocal cords before a performance.

While you're warming up your Actor, you're also gathering important information about the social environment you're in and the people you're dealing with. Each social encounter will build upon the next to increase your self-confidence and knowledge, en route to helping you connect with the person of your dreams.

Exercise 4. Building Up Your Social Comfort Zone

In this exercise you will extend your comfort zone by gradually building upon each social encounter you engage in. You will begin with the least threatening interactions and build up to the most challenging—and potentially rewarding—ones.

STEP 1. As soon as you walk into a social situation, take the time to observe everyone there (check out Chapter 10 for tips on how to read people in social situations). Try to determine who looks open and receptive to conversation and who doesn't. Decide who appears popular and surrounded by people, and who seems lonely, uncomfortable, or left out. Count all the service staff, if any: the bartenders, waiters, waitresses, and so forth. If it's a private party, take note of the host or hostess and where he or she is.

STEP 2. As you relax and center yourself in the Tan Tien (see the previous two exercises), focus on the first person you'd like to converse with. This will be your initial warm-up person: the least threatening man or woman in the room, the easiest one to talk to. Your goal when speaking with this person is to catch a good vibe and begin to feel comfortable and accepted in the social setting.

When you've selected your first conversational partner, walk over to him or her with your best smile and begin a short conversation. Perhaps you'll make a comment to the bartender about how big the crowd is tonight, or maybe you'll ask the hostess for directions to a good post-party diner. Keep the questions simple and the conversation brief. Your goal here is to warm up your conversational muscles a bit and experience an instant feeling of acceptance: Someone is actually talking to you and responding in a positive and friendly way.

STEP 3. Next find that stranger who appears to be out of the social loop, someone who looks a bit lonely, awkward, or Introverted. Be careful here: You don't want people who seem too depressed or resigned; their bad attitude may rub off on you. Instead, find someone who may be a little plain-looking or shy but whose eyes dart around the room in anticipation, whose body language (see Chapter 10 for clues) signals a desire to meet someone new.

Now summon up your courage and approach Ms. Plain Jane or Mr. Average Bob. Begin a conversation, or better yet, if there's music, ask him or her to dance. Relax. There's no pressure here; the first one doesn't count. This is simply your warm-up person—there are no expectations for either of you to like each other. Simply enjoy the good energy this person may give you and move on from there.

You may be surprised: Sometimes the first one can be the best. If you look beyond surface appearance, you may find that the two of you really hit it off. If that's the case, you may want to stay with that person for the rest of the evening. Consider yourself lucky: You've just encountered that rarity of social occurrences—instant rapport and connection.

STEP 4. If the warm-up person isn't your type, continue interacting with the rest of the people at the event who appear open,
friendly, and interested in making a connection, or at least in making
conversation.

Your goal at this stage is not to win someone's approval, get a
phone number or date, or meet your soul mate. It's simply to become increasingly comfortable and warmed up to the social environment until you feel you can talk with the most attractive person
in the room without experiencing a great deal of anxiety and embarrassment.

Have fun with this exercise and see how far you can go in meeting
the people you want to meet, without carrying any expectations.
Your only goal here is to warm up your social muscles gradually and
have a great time. Ironically, the more loose and relaxed you are in
social situations, the more likely you are to meet and attract the person you really want.

The Best Gift You Can Give Yourself

At its essence warming up is a supreme act of self-compassion and
self-love. It is you saying to you: I'm a delicate and sensitive person
who deserves to feel safe and protected. I'm not going to rush myself; I'm not going to throw myself into a social situation that will
pressure or overwhelm me.

When you give yourself the gift of warming up, you will no longer
thrust yourself into potentially harsh social environments without
adequate preparation. You will no longer criticize yourself because
you're not instantly charming and successful in potential romantic
encounters. You will, instead, be patient with yourself. You will take
the steps you need—relaxing yourself, centering yourself in your
Tan Tien, and having practice conversations—to get yourself ready
to go out and excel in the social world. In time you will settle into
the perfect comfort zone that protects your sensitive, delicate nature and gives you the confidence to be at your all-time best.

CHAPTER 7

Getting Your Fools Out

Sherry, a shy thirty-one-year-old retail manager, had to admit it: She was secretly envious of her co-worker Callista's love life. For as long as Sherry had known her, forty-nine-year-old Callista had been a man magnet—attracting incredible-looking men at a record-breaking pace. Sherry had no clue how Callista did it. Callista wasn't particularly attractive—actually she was thirty pounds overweight and at least ten years older than she cared to admit. But she always managed to have an attractive, intelligent, and successful boyfriend who treated her like a queen. Sherry, meanwhile, had only a couple of broken relationships—partners she could graciously call underachievers and not so graciously call losers—to show for her many years of dating.

When Callista brought her latest flame, an adoring thirty-five-year-old Ricky Martin look-alike, to the store, Sherry just about lost it. Although she was embarrassed to ask her, she had to know Callista's secret. "I don't have a secret, not really," said an amused Callista when Sherry approached her after Ricky Jr. had tangoed out of the store. "In fact, I'm still kind of shy with men. People don't realize this, but I've always been shy."

"Then how do you do it?" asked an amazed Sherry. She had never thought of Callista as shy.

"Long ago, I learned a simple mental trick," said Callista. "I knew I had this fun-loving personality inside me, but my shyness didn't let me get it out. I was always too afraid of looking like a fool to be spontaneous and wacky the way I wanted to be. But then I learned how to get my fools out."

"Your fools?"

"I call them my fools—the fun, spontaneous, and crazy stuff inside me. Once I started getting them out, men really responded. Now guys are calling me all the time, and I'm having way too much fun."

It sounded kind of weird and a little scary, but it was definitely worth a try, thought Sherry. Especially if she could nab a Leonardo DiCaprio look-alike for herself. Yes, that would work; getting her fools out was already starting to sound like a really good idea.

You know what it takes to be truly spontaneous? It's just one simple thing: the willingness to risk looking like a fool. The courage to put yourself out there no matter what, regardless of what others may think; the ability to have fun and not take your social performance so damn seriously. In ImprovTherapy terms this is known as getting your fools out—expressing all your spontaneous and fun-loving thoughts, feelings, and instincts, giving yourself permission to be authentic, creative, funny, and unique.

In other words, to be the real You.

As a shy person, you probably have hundreds of inner fools you've never expressed because you were afraid of what people might think. Inside you lives that straitlaced high school student who wanted to heave water balloons on the last day of senior year but was too scared to do it. There's that shy woman who was dying to write "You're cute" in lipstick on that gorgeous guy's napkin, but was too shy to go through with it.

The irony here is that the more you try to prevent your fools from emerging, the more likely they are to come out and embarrass you in the worst ways possible.

When you try to exert tight control over your fools—in a frantic attempt to avoid embarrassment—you often create the opposite effect: You bring forth the fools. There they come, just as you're about to ask that dream person for a date, just when that gorgeous stranger offers to buy you a drink. It happens every time: The more you try to avoid embarrassment, the more embarrassment comes to get you.

By contrast, when you express your fools fully, you will savor that deliciously liberating feeling that comes when you no longer care what others think. You know that, as long as you don't hurt anyone, it's OK to be spontaneous and have fun. When you get your fools out in the right way, you will enjoy a tremendous confidence boost. Instead of trying so hard to impress others, you will relax and let the conversation come to you. As you release your fools, you will declare: "I don't care if I make a social mistake, or even if someone thinks I'm being foolish. I embrace my fools—the silly, natural, fun-loving, and sometimes foolish parts of me. I know that every fool I express will bring me one step closer to achieving my full romantic potential."

Always remember that getting your fools out is not about embarrassing yourself or others; it's not about making fun of other people, or yourself for that matter. You will maintain your respectful, shy-sensitive side; you will still use your Observer to make sure you don't step over the line and do something inappropriate or disrespectful.

Your goal in getting your fools out is to become a mature Actor, someone who can express his or her naturally fun and spontaneous side—joking, clowning, posing, singing, and dancing—while at the same time bringing much-needed goodwill, sensitivity, and compassion into the world.

When you think about getting your fools out, don't worry that you have to get them out all at once, or that you have to get them out in public in the beginning. In the following exercises you will learn how to acknowledge and release these feisty, fun-loving creatures at your own pace, in the privacy of your home or in a quiet, secluded setting.

As you gain more practice and confidence releasing your fools in private, you will want to liven up your social life by incorporating fool work into your daily routine. Maybe you will tell a spicy joke to a small group of close friends; perhaps you will improvise a story in front of some co-workers. Whatever you do, make sure it's slightly outside your comfort level—not so easy that it doesn't challenge you and not so difficult that you feel you're in way over your head.

Let the Fools Rush In:
Spontaneity in Action

After getting rid of his father's condemning Observer, Katsu felt like the whole world was his candy store. He had a blast getting his fools out everywhere he went—in front of store clerks, waitresses, and gas station attendants. The beauty of it all was that there was no judgment or evaluation in anything he did. Getting his fools out was the only thing that mattered.

Brimming with confidence, Katsu decided to try his fool-releasing strategy on Carolyn, one of the most beautiful women he had ever seen—a heart-melting, brown-eyed, thirty-nine-year-old research manager who worked in another division of his company. After asking a mutual friend to introduce them, Katsu prepped himself with the idea that no matter what happened he would get his fools out and make internal progress. He couldn't lose.

When he met Carolyn for smoothies at a nearby yogurt shop, he immediately noticed her attractive tiger print outfit. "There's a tiger loose around here," said Katsu as soon as the thought popped into his mind. He instantly blushed a little—normally he wouldn't be so bold with a woman as beautiful as Carolyn.

"But I'm not wild," replied Carolyn as she lit up the place with her deliciously intoxicating laugh. She loved a sense of humor in a smart man.

"You know, my insurance only covers pussycats," said a fool-spewing Katsu as he decided to go for broke. "Tigers are a little extra."

"That's OK; I'm worth it," replied Carolyn as she started warming up to Katsu. He was funny *and* kind of cute. "Meowww."

Katsu almost swallowed his straw, but he was able to recover in time to ask Carolyn out to the movies. They enjoyed a double feature the next night and started dating seriously. Thirteen months later, they moved in together and have been deeply in love ever since. Now Katsu and Carolyn have plenty of time to get their fools out together as they romp like delighted schoolchildren and make love like wild animals.

Are you afraid to let your fools out? Don't be; they exist only to bring you fun and pleasure, joy and exuberance. With the help of these irresistible creatures, you'll be able to turn up the romantic volume and revitalize your love life.

Don't worry about going too far and making a real fool out of yourself. The Observer—your old watchdog—will still be there watching your back, no matter what. You can always count on the Observer to be the safety net that keeps you within the boundaries of polite society and good taste. You will never do anything really rude or obnoxious as long as the Observer is watching you, serving as your social conscience.

When you release your fools, you will come to the fantastic realization that everything is possible in your social life. You have just done one of the riskiest, scariest things imaginable: You have exposed your most primitive thoughts, feelings, and impulses—your fools—to the world, and you have survived. Not only have you survived but you have thrived. You have brought fun and joy to yourself and others, and you have expressed your true nature. Now others will be irresistibly attracted to you because they will see you as a genuine individual who is comfortable in your own skin and who is not afraid to be spontaneous and carefree when the time is right.

Exercise 1. Say Hello to Your Spontaneous Side

Before you release your fools, it's a good idea to become acquainted with your spontaneous urges, impulses, and feelings in a private and comfortable setting. Here you will explore the hidden parts of yourself.

STEP 1. Begin to wander around your house, moving from room to room as the urge strikes you. Don't plan where you're going to go; just let your mind take over and move you.

STEP 2. Continue walking around your house, except this time express your feelings about the items and objects you observe. Don't use any words to describe your feelings, simply express yourself through sounds and nonverbal gestures. You may, for example, stomp your feet and grimace when you see your alarm clock; you may clap your hands and smile in delight as you come across your daughter's baby pictures.

STEP 3. Repeat Step 2, except this time add words to your reactions. You may say: "Damn, I hate alarm clocks," or "I love my daughter," as you respond to your home environment.

The more you become attuned to the natural rhythms of your mind, the more you will be able to access your spontaneous Actor and respond authentically to each moment you experience.

Exercise 2. Releasing Your Fools

Now that you're becoming more aware of your natural instincts and feelings, it's time to let your fools come out and play. In this exercise you will release your fools and bring much-needed fun and energy into your social repertoire.

STEP 1. Find a cozy, quiet, and private place—perhaps your bedroom, backyard, or a secluded spot in nature. This will be your fool-releasing space. Wear loose clothing—sweats, for example—that allows you to move about freely and comfortably. Make sure the clothes are old and won't be a great loss if they get damaged or dirty.

STEP 2. In this safe, private place, decide that you will get as wild, crazy, spontaneous, and just plain nuts as you possibly can. Make faces, jump up and down, scream, pick your nose, shake your rear, roar like a lion, get on all fours like a donkey, roll all over the grass, put mud on your face. Your aim is to be totally silly and spontaneous, and let your fools bust loose.

STEP 3. Continue these crazy antics until you completely tire yourself out. Now collapse to the ground and just lie there. Hear your heart beat, pay attention to your feelings. Write down what you're thinking and feeling; record any insights you may have gained by doing this exercise.

STEP 4. Bring your fool-releasing work to the outside world. Tell a joke to a co-worker, sing a little louder at church, laugh a bit harder than usual, heave some water balloons at a friend, make mud pies with the neighborhood children. Stay within your comfort level at first—get your fools out with a third-grader or a friend you trust—and eventually spread your wings: Get your fools out in front of neighbors, strangers, anybody.

When you let your fools come out and play, you will realize just how much fun and passion you can generate. You will think: Why didn't I release my fools earlier? I could have enjoyed a much more rewarding social life. It's not too late. Starting today, resolve to get your fools out on a daily basis. Just like building muscles, getting your fools out is a gradual process that will yield excellent results over time.

Exercise 3. Fool Jumping: Excitement as Spontaneity

Jenny, a seventeen-year-old high school senior, had her eye on Steve, an eighteen-year-old buff hottie and member of the swim team. She definitely wanted to get next to her crush, but her shyness kept her from doing anything about it. Jenny was really sad because she knew they would be graduating soon, and she was about to miss the opportunity of a lifetime.

Luckily for Jenny, she had a best bud in Tamika, who gave her the encouragement she needed: "Jenny, you gotta get some rah-rah into your love life. You need some excitement and enthusiasm when it comes to hooking up with guys. Your fools gotta come out, girl-friend."

Following Tamika's advice, Jenny found a comfortable place where she could get her fools out. She imagined all the things that made her happy and excited—especially all the fun she could have with that cutie Steve if she got to know him better—as she jumped up and down, yelling, laughing, and shifting her excitement level into high gear.

As her enthusiasm and confidence grew, Jenny started to do little things to catch Steve's eye: smiling at him when they passed each other in the hall, asking him questions about the swim team, and of-fering to study with him (she was, after all, the top student in their AP English class).

On his end, Steve enjoyed hanging out with Jenny; she was super-funny and really smart. Plus she wasn't bad-looking either. Before long Jenny and Steve went on their first official date, and now they're really into each other. They're looking forward to kickin' it all summer and keeping their flame burning bright.

There's an element of excitement in spontaneity. Pure, unfettered joy—helium rising, fireworks exploding, clouds opening up, reaching that peak of ecstasy and coming back for more. We call this the rah-rah factor, the raw high of undiluted social excitement, the pure pleasure that comes from socializing and having fun in the dating world.

Many shy people, unfortunately, take a vacation from social excitement and allow themselves to become dull over time. They may show some excitement and enthusiasm when they're with close friends, but they will rarely release the same energy in a social environment. Instead of being alive with excitement, many shy people hunker down in the corner, avoiding eye contact, their speech slow and empty (or fast and mumbled), afraid to stand out, petrified of saying the wrong things and looking like fools.

It's no wonder that many shy people are dead on their feet in social settings. They often go home early and complain that they are tired and lack energy. They are tired because they suppress their own energy, their own excitement. They follow the Observer's lead when it tells them they must be extremely careful and vigilant in social situations: "Don't be too loud, too excited, too much of anything; don't stand out and embarrass yourself. Just be your same low-profile, plain vanilla self. Slink into that corner and evaporate like water in August. There, that's not so bad."

By now you know better than to listen to the already muted Observer. Rather than pay attention to this vanishing creature, why don't you unleash your rah-rah power—all your hidden excitement and joy—and express it right here, right now?

STEP 1. Find a comfortable and private place where you can make all the noise you want. You may want to use your bedroom, backyard, garage, or a secluded nature setting.

STEP 2. Think of all the enjoyable things in your life, all the fun and exciting things that have ever happened to you: getting the first job you really wanted, driving your first car, having your first wonderful sexual and romantic experience. As you think of these things (if you can't think of any, imagine what your most exciting experience would be like), start saying the word *yes* aloud to yourself.

STEP 3. Continue saying yes as you gradually build up your excitement level. Get louder, funkier, and more excited: Jump, dance, mug, give yourself a high five. Let yourself go. Feel the absolute joy, passion, and pleasure of the word—YES—with all its hidden connotations:

YES is the expression of all your possibilities, of all the great fun social times you can, and will, have—of all the intimacy, passion, and love you will enjoy with your treasured mate.

YES is the spaceship that bursts through the gravity of social fears and rejections and takes you into the rare air of romantic mastery, into the universe of unconditional social success.

Say it now, say it loud: yes, yes, Yes, YES, YES, YESS!!!!! YESS-SSSSSS!!!!!!!!

With this exercise as your guide, you will bring a newfound sense of enthusiasm and excitement into your dating life. When you walk into a room, you will automatically generate a buzz of excitement as others look at you and say simply: Wow!

Exercise 4. Fool Crashing: Telling It Like It Is

We've saved the best for last. The most challenging, yes. The most rewarding, definitely. This is where you put away everything you've learned about politeness and reserved behavior and allow yourself to express fully what you truly think and feel. In this exercise you will learn how to communicate your innermost thoughts, feelings, and instincts—your fools—directly and honestly, regardless of what others may think.

No, you won't become a scoundrel, sociopath, or mean person when you do this. What you *will* do is handcuff your Observer for a moment, just to see what it's like to express your deeply held feelings—even raw and difficult ones—without worrying so much about what others think. You will let a person know he or she hurt you if that is what happened. You will tell someone he or she is acting like a jerk if that's the way it is.

You may think this is brash, impolite, or even aggressive, but in reality it's the pure honest truth. Sure, it's possible to go too far and be rude and obnoxious, but you're unlikely to do that if you're a shy person. Chances are, you go the other way: You sugarcoat your true feelings and don't express them because you're afraid of hurting people and losing their friendship. Think of all the years you've wasted tiptoeing around people, afraid of saying the wrong things, overly concerned with trying to make others like you. What has this gotten you so far? Chances are, it has made you timid and afraid of being yourself and speaking your mind.

Of course, there's nothing wrong with trying to fit in and pleasing other people. Treating people well and promoting social harmony are good things. The problem comes when you try to please others at your own expense—when you sacrifice your true nature, your emotional integrity, in a futile attempt to win someone's approval and affections.

Here's some news: That person you're trying to win over with your fake moves probably won't like you much anyway. Nobody likes phonies, and that's exactly what you are when you go against your grain to try to win someone's love instead of living fully from your center. Even if you succeed in fooling that person with your act, guess what happens when he or she discovers the real you. That's right, trouble.

When you hold yourself back from being your true self, you harm yourself and those around you. Think about it: Have you ever damaged a relationship because you didn't speak up when you should have? Chances are, if you had been more direct and straightforward with your feelings earlier on, you could have salvaged the relationship. Yet no matter what has happened to you in the past, you're about to get a second chance. In this exercise you will learn how to express your most deeply held thoughts, opinions, and feelings. Once you're able to do this, you will take a quantum leap toward developing social mastery.

STEP 1. Think of something you've wanted to say to a friend or colleague for a while but have been too shy to do so. Perhaps a co-worker made a mean remark that hurt you. You didn't say anything at the time, but you've been wanting to clear the air about it. Or maybe you've been wanting to tell your friend how much you appreciate his or her friendship, but you've been too embarrassed to speak up.

STEP 2. Get in front of a mirror, and stand with your feet shoulder width apart and your arms at your sides. Imagine that your entire identity is centered in your Tan Tien as you breathe deeply and feel its power, energy, and vitality spreading through your entire body.

STEP 3. Visualize the person you've wanted to say something to as he or she stands before you in the mirror. Imagine that this individual has a warm and accepting face that will embrace whatever you have to say.

STEP 4. Look your friend or colleague in the eye, and speak your mind.

If you stumble over your words, don't fret. If your phrasing isn't perfect, don't stress. Your goal here is not to be supersmooth or persuade this person to agree with everything you're saying. Your only task is to express your innermost feelings directly and honestly, without censoring or interrupting yourself.

STEP 5. Practice this exercise in the mirror until you're confident enough to approach your friend or acquaintance in person. When you're face-to-face with this individual, wait until the time is right—then raise the topic you've been rehearsing. Resolve that, no matter how anxious you feel, you will do everything possible to say what needs to be said.

In the beginning you may express yourself in small matters: "Where's the twenty dollars I lent you six months ago?" Then, as you gain more comfort and confidence, you can begin to assert yourself in bigger and more important areas: "I resent the way you treated me in front of my friends."

You can't imagine the liberating and joyous feelings you will experience when you finally let your fools out—when you allow yourself to express your truest feelings and opinions without being petrified that you will be criticized, embarrassed, or rejected. When you're open authentically like this, your friend or colleague may not agree with everything you're saying, but he or she will most likely respect your right to say it. And, more often than not, this person will be on your side, apologizing for past mistakes and offering support and encouragement.

Expressing your innermost feelings may not always be easy or socially desirable, but it's one of the best ways to build your self-confidence. When you know you're capable of communicating the most challenging and volatile feelings to someone, anything else you say to that individual (or to anyone else, for that matter) will be a piece of cake.

That's not all. By expressing your feelings directly in this way, you've established yourself as a genuine person who speaks the truth. In a world filled with dishonest creeps and lying fakes, a person who speaks from his or her heart is a marvel, both priceless and rare.

The Fools Aren't Really Dunces, They're Straight-A Students

By now you may be getting the idea: There's nothing dumb or stupid about the fools. Actually, they are socially intelligent entities that can give you a tremendous edge in the dating world. When you allow the natural and spicy parts of you to surface, others will be amazed by your social brilliance and awed by the fact that you can be such a nice, easygoing person and still possess the fire, chemistry, and charisma most often found in very outgoing, Extraverted people.

Sure, you may go overboard occasionally and say something a bit too silly, but you know how to recover quickly. You know it's only another fool coming out; it's no reflection on you or your social worthiness. You realize your fools are not out to hurt or embarrass anyone; they exist only to bring joy, fun, and honesty to the world as you develop your social skills and skyrocket your romantic confidence.

Long live the fools.

CHAPTER 8

Communicating with Your Entire Essence

Johnny, a divorced forty-four-year-old Irish American financial consultant, and a big bear of a man at six feet four and 260 pounds, talked way too much. He knew it, but he couldn't help himself, especially when he was in the presence of an attractive woman he wanted to impress.

Perfect example: At last year's Christmas office party, Johnny was standing next to a real cute co-worker named Alice when he unleashed a mile-a-minute monologue about his all-time favorite hobby: chess. "Fischer was just fantastic, but Kasparov was even better," Johnny proclaimed as he tapped Alice on the shoulder for emphasis. "And the two of them playing against each other would have been a match made in heaven. How about you, Alice, have you ever played chess? Would you like to play with me sometime?"

Yes, Alice had played chess before, but she didn't care much for the game. And she was equally put off by Johnny's rapid-fire speech and pushy style. As soon as Johnny cornered her, she was looking for a way out, and thank God she found it when one of her girlfriends came over to ask her a question.

Although he didn't show it at the time, Johnny was hurt. In reality, he wasn't the aggressive brute some people thought he was. Deep down, he was just a big shy cuddly bear who wanted approval and love from everyone, especially women. His problem was that he tried too hard to make women like him, and instead of showing his soft, caring nature, he displayed the opposite: an overbearing man-ner that pushed women away.

Johnny realized he needed help, but he didn't know where to look or what he might find when he got there. He had been this way a long time, and he knew change wouldn't come easily.

If you had X-ray vision, you could easily spot a shy person at a party: the eager-to-please person buried under an avalanche of so-cial expectations; the tortured soul driven by the erroneous idea that he or she must be uncommonly suave, smooth, and Extravert, or else. Or else no one will like the shy person, and he or she will never win the affections of that dream mate.

As the shy person buckles under the weight of unrealistic expec-tations, one of two things can happen. First, the shy person will try too hard to make a favorable impression. Like Johnny, the shy indi-vidual will let loose with an inappropriate barrage of boring chit-chat and interrogating questions in a vain attempt to impress the appealing person. Unfortunately, this kamikaze strategy often back-fires and creates the opposite effect: It pushes others away and leaves the shy person standing alone, wondering what went wrong. The other likelihood is that the shy person will collapse under this self-created mental pressure. Rather than risk embarrassment, the shy person will retreat into a shell and fade away into obscurity.

If an attractive person should look toward the shy person, timid Tom or shy Suzy would avoid eye contact. If that sexy stranger should happen to come over and start a conversation, the shy person would speak sparingly and hope he or she would leave soon.

Even though this retreat and disappear strategy may work well to protect the shy person from embarrassment in the short run, it cre-ates more pain in the end. After the aborted encounter, the shy person's Observer kicks in: Why didn't you talk more to that inter-esting person? Why are you such a coward? You really blew it this time, big time.

You may have fallen into this trap hundreds of times in the past, but things are about to change. You're about to learn a simple but re-markable truth:

YOU DON'T HAVE TO BE A GREAT CONVERSATIONALIST TO WIN SOMEONE'S HEART. TO ATTRACT THE PERSON OF YOUR DREAMS, ALL YOU HAVE TO DO IS BE YOURSELF.

In this chapter you will learn how to project an alluring and exciting romantic presence by being your shy-sensitive self and using the versatile nonverbal tools of silence, action, and space. With these powerful dynamics as your guides, your entire social outlook will change. Whereas before you felt pressured to say the right thing all the time, now you can simply relax and let the words come to you naturally as you set the stage first with your nonverbal presence.

Although shy people have a lot to offer, society doesn't always encourage them to embrace their natural strengths. In Western society especially, too much emphasis is placed on verbal communication as the only way to make social and romantic connections.

Consider, for example, the dating courses and self-help books that are popular in the West. Many of these programs emphasize clever small talk strategies and manipulative pickup lines designed to win someone's heart or get into his or her pants. Not only are these approaches superficial and manipulative but they're often ineffective because people can see right through them.

What's worse, shy people who follow these programs often feel even more pressure to excel verbally. They think: If I'm not as verbally smooth and conversationally charming as these courses and books tell me to be, I will never date and find true love.

Hogwash. Although words are important (you'll learn the best ways to express yourself verbally in the next chapter), the truth is that you can communicate a great deal about yourself through your actions, nonverbal expressions, and use of physical space.

You can take a clue from Japanese society and the way they express themselves through subtle signs, customs, and rituals: through the beautiful tea ceremony, flower arrangements, poetry (haiku), and calligraphy (shodo). All of these activities can reflect the emotional mood of Japanese as well as, or better than, verbal communication. If a Japanese wife is angry at her husband, for example, she may not say anything directly to him. She may, instead, misarrange several flowers in a vase. When her husband arrives he will see the out-of-place flowers and realize his wife is upset.

When it comes to Japanese courtship, the actual words spoken are not as important as where and how two people meet, where they sit and how well they listen, how much poise they have, and how responsive they are to each other's needs and interests. According to the Japanese, these are the true gauges of a relationship, often more valuable and important in determining romantic compatibility than what the partners say to each other. In the ImprovTherapy approach, you will adopt the Japanese sense of subtlety and detail to help you develop a romantic presence without having to rely too much on words to make your point.

Silence: The Language of Love

Oscar, a handsome and athletic twenty-one-year-old business major, had a strong liking for Lucinda, a petite, twenty-year-old education major who sat in the back of their psychology class. Although Lucinda wasn't what anyone would call a babe, there was something about her quiet and deep-thinking nature that really impressed Oscar and made him want to get close to her.

Lucinda was the type of girl who rarely said anything in class, but when she did, it was always something deep. The teacher would praise her input, and others in the class would join in a lively discussion based on Lucinda's comments. But it wasn't just her smarts that attracted Oscar; it was Lucinda's calm and soft-spoken personality that sealed the deal. After class they would sit and talk, or just sit quietly together without saying anything. Oscar always felt soothed by Lucinda's quiet nature, and he felt really comfortable with her.

As a popular member of the top fraternity on campus, Oscar knew a lot of girls who were attracted to him, but he wanted Lucinda. Oscar realized he would break some hearts if he got serious with Lucinda, but he had to go for what he felt was right: Lucinda, the quiet girl, was definitely the one.

There's a beauty in quietness, a wonder in stillness. To be with someone and not have to say anything is one of the most enjoyable parts of an intimate relationship. But silence is not only for a couple in love; it can also play an important role in all stages of dating and romance.

When you use silence in the right way, you can communicate a fascinating array of emotions and attitudes: the cool, misty silence of mystery and intrigue, the hot-flamed silence of sexy self-confidence, and the sun-warmed silence of really listening to another human being. For shy people, silence is an excellent way to convey thoughts and emotions that mere words can't describe. Although there are times when shy people need to break out of their silence and speak up, there are many opportunities for shy people to make a powerful statement by using silence in an intelligent and creative manner.

In Western society, unfortunately, many people are uncomfortable with silence. They feel compelled to fill in the gaps with idle talk and empty chatter. Japanese society, on the other hand, considers silence one of the highest forms of communication. In Japan silence is prized as a positive state that creates openness and a flow of energy between people and allows them to reach into their deeper personal resources. Statements such as "A flower does not speak," and "The mouth is to eat with, not to speak with," are used in Japan because silence is seen not as a handicap but as a worthy complement to verbal communication.

In one interesting study researchers investigated the differences between Japanese and American attitudes toward silence. They showed sketches of expressionless faces (in various social settings) to Japanese and Americans to see how they would interpret silences of various lengths. Americans in the study interpreted the faces as being full of worry, criticism, regret, or embarrassment, while Japanese saw them more as indicating a neutral waiting period or evidence of agreement.

As a shy person you already have the skill of silence in your social repertoire. Chances are you've used silence a great deal in your past social encounters. The problem was that you probably didn't appreciate the beauty and power of silence. Rather than seeing it as the dynamic and multifaceted form of communication it is, you chastised yourself for being weak and limited because you didn't speak out like the more outgoing and talkative people of the world.

Begin today to see your quiet nature as an asset instead of a liability. Treasure your silence as the secret weapon that can transform your shy personality into a powerful love magnet—effortlessly attracting the people you want to meet.

Exercise 1. Silent Empathy

Have you ever sat silently with a close friend and felt what he or she was feeling? If so, you have experienced silent empathy: the ability to experience what other people are feeling without needing to communicate verbally. In this exercise you will learn how to improve your social relationships by using silent empathy in your daily encounters. Here's what you do.

STEP 1. Choose a partner, and sit approximately two feet away from him or her. Ask your partner to focus on a situation that created a strong feeling in him or her, whether anger, sadness, joy, excitement, or the like. Have your partner visualize the situation in detail and reexperience the strong emotion that accompanied it.

STEP 2. As you look at your partner, imagine that there is a solid white line of energy that connects your Tan Tien to your partner's. Visualize that you're traveling along this energy passageway into your partner's Tan Tien. See yourself sitting in your friend's Tan Tien as you experience life from his or her emotional perspective.

STEP 3. From this new viewpoint, write down the emotion you feel your friend is experiencing and the situation that triggered it. Ask your friend what he or she was experiencing, and see how accurate your conclusions were.

STEP 4. Whenever you go out, focus on connecting with other people—Tan Tien to Tan Tien—as you access their emotional nature.

When you do this your whole attitude toward people will change: Whereas before you may have been fearful, anxious, and self-conscious, now you will experience life from their perspective, and you will no longer be afraid of them. You will recognize the truth: It's impossible to be afraid of someone when you experience life as that person. When you become that individual for a moment, there is no separation, no threat, nothing to fear.

Exercise 2. Become the Quiet Romantic

Silence is a versatile dating tool that can evoke a wide variety of attractive and desirable romantic qualities. In this exercise you will learn how to incorporate silence into your daily life as a multifaceted romantic asset.

STEP 1. Think of an intriguing image or emotion you would like to convey, such as mystery, calmness, strength of mind, integrity, or sexy self-confidence.

STEP 2. Find a practice conversational partner, and begin a conversation. Concentrate on using silence to convey whatever emotion or trait you selected in Step 1. If, for example, you chose sexy self-confidence, you may answer your partner's question with a pause followed by a playful smile or wink. If you decided to convey deep thinking, you may remain silent as you put your thumb on your chin and your index finger on your nose in the classic thinker's pose.

STEP 3. Use silence in your daily conversations. Chances are, you're already quite conversationally fluent with your friends, so it may be somewhat of a challenge for you to slow down, pause, and remain silent for longer periods when you're with them. Your friends may wonder why you're acting differently, but simply tell them you're working on an exercise in silent communication.

STEP 4. Incorporate silence into your social repertoire, and use it with the new people you meet. Rather than stuff your conversation with extraneous and meaningless words, let silence float in at the appropriate moments to evoke the mood you want to convey, whether it be curiosity, intrigue, confidence, or anything else.

Action: The Spark That Lights Your Romantic Fire

A hunk he wasn't. Successful in his career? Not that. Smooth talker? No way. Yet Charles, a balding, overweight thirty-nine-year-old painter, somehow managed to be extraordinarily successful with beautiful women. Without trying, it seemed, Charles always knew at least two or three gorgeous women who were crazy about him.

Charles's secret was actually quite simple: He did little things to help people and make them feel better. He was always the first to light a cigarette, hold open a door, offer advice and help. Charles even had his eye out on the freeway for stalled cars; he had met his last girlfriend after she got a flat tire and he helped her change it.

Although Charles was usually too shy to say much to a woman he helped, he found that the grateful lady would often do a lot of the talking, and he could exercise another one of his great talents: listening. Women really loved telling him their problems, and he was more than eager to lend a sympathetic ear and make a new friend.

If only Charles's shy friends would catch on, they too could enjoy active and fulfilling romantic lives. Unfortunately, his friends were too caught up in their own feelings of frustration and resentment to notice what Charles was doing. They spent most of their time trying to meet women on the Internet and lamenting their lousy love lives.

Too bad, thought Charles. It's so easy to connect with people if you just focus on doing a few simple caring things for them. It's so natural; everyone ought to be doing it.

Here's some good news: If you want to excel in the dating game, you don't need to make flamboyant romantic gestures. You don't need to engage in movie-quality flirtatious dialogue or act in outrageously seductive ways. All you have to do are a few simple things that express your true personality and bring you closer to people. Smile at someone, hold a door open for a stranger, or offer someone a pen to write with. These are the simple, subtle behaviors that create goodwill and give you the opportunity to connect with others in a positive way.

When your social life is made up of easy, good-natured, bite-size movements, a tremendous weight is lifted off your shoulders. You no longer need to suffer under huge social expectations. You no longer need to worry about always having to impress, please, or win someone over with your persuasive and charming words. You understand the meaning of the statement "Words are like the stem, and movement is like the flower." As a shy person, you can communicate a great deal without having to say a lot, simply by expressing your-self through the small gestures and kindnesses you offer those around you.

Exercise 3. Look Who's Knocking

There are many ways to communicate without using words. In this exercise you will communicate who you are by doing some-thing as simple as knocking on a door.

STEP 1. Ask a friend to help by listening carefully as you knock on a door. Your friend will try to guess what kind of person you are and what's on your mind based on the way you knock.

STEP 2. Decide on a character you want to play and something he or she wants. He may be an angry husband who has been kicked out of the house and demands to come in. She may be a flirtatious damsel who has arrived with a sexy surprise for her beloved.

STEP 3. Go outside your home and knock on your door as your character. If you're playing the angry husband, for example, you may pound on the door heavily and quickly like a rat-tat-tat machine gun. If you're acting like the flirtatious maiden, you may tap lightly a few times, pause, then tap a few more, as if you were sending a sexy signal in Morse code. You won't say any words when you do this; your only communication will be the knock.

SPECIAL TIP. This exercise will remind you to use the most subtle actions to communicate important information about yourself and what you want from the social world. If, for example, you want to appear sexy and inviting, stir the straw sensually in your drink when your potential love object is looking at you. If you want to project kindness and compassion, offer a tired person your seat. If you want to display rapt attention and self-confidence, hold eye contact for a couple of seconds longer than usual.

When you use these subtle actions to convey powerful messages about your desires, you will no longer have to worry about stum-bling over your words and saying the wrong things. Your actions will do all the communicating for you.

Exercise 4. Let Your Feet Do the Talking

In this exercise you will learn how to use something other than your mouth to communicate; you will let your feet do the talking.

STEP 1. Lie on the floor and have your partner cover you completely with a blanket, except for your feet.

STEP 2. Think of an emotion you would like to convey using only your feet. You will not use any other part of your body, and you will not speak.

STEP 3. Convey the emotion solely with your feet. You may communicate with happy feet that tap and bounce around, shy feet that cower on the edges of the blanket, scared to stick out all the way, or sexy feet that do a hot strip dance and signal "I want your sole."

SPECIAL TIP. Learn how to communicate with your entire body. Think, feel, and act from every portion of your body: Cry with your stomach, get sexy with your elbow, love from your feet. When you communicate through different parts of your body like this, you will immediately relieve a great deal of pent-up tension and anxiety.

Because shy people tend to place their entire focus on their mouths, they put an enormous amount of pressure on themselves to say the right thing. It's no surprise, then, that shy people have a tendency to cover up their mouths, worry about mouth odor, and stutter and stumble over their words. For shy people, their incapable and incompetent mouths are the perfect symbols of their social inadequacy.

Instead of relying on your mouth so much, try communicating with different parts of your body. If you want to feel confident and sexy, put your focus on your Tan Tien. If you want to feel silly and funny, concentrate on your nose or butt. As you communicate with your entire body in this way, you will notice a dramatic improvement in your self-confidence and social results. Others will be strongly attracted to you because you project a presence that is dynamic, well-balanced, and multifaceted.

Exercise 5. What Are We Doing?

This is an energetic exercise that involves several people and demonstrates the power of communicating without words and working together as a group. Several actors will participate in an activity without speaking (pantomime), while the audience tries to guess what the actors are doing by interpreting their gestures, expressions, and movements.

STEP 1. Choose a minimum of three people who will be the actors (you will be one of them) and include at least three others who will make up the audience.

The actors will confer for a few minutes to choose a group activity. Avoid sports and spectator activities (watching TV, for example). Better choices include active joint behaviors, such as doing the dishes or building a house. The scenes should be simple and realistic (avoid high-fantasy concepts such as building a Plutonian spaceship).

STEP 2. The first person in the group will come to the stage (front of the room) and begin the activity.

STEP 3. The other members will join the action one by one until everyone is working together. Members of the audience will then try to guess what the activity is. Once someone gets it right, the scene is over.

Check to see that all the members of the group are doing the same activity. Sometimes one person will start acting independently, and the group will need to bring him or her back in line with the group activity. Also, make sure that no words are spoken during the exercise; it will be done strictly in pantomime.

VARIATION. Repeat the exercise, except this time with no prearranged group or preselected activity. This time someone from the audience will come up onstage spontaneously and begin doing the first activity that comes to mind. When someone in the audience thinks he or she knows what the actor is doing, that person will join the activity. More people will come up until everyone knows the activity and is doing it onstage. Again, no words will be spoken during the exercise.

SPECIAL TIP. The next time you're at a social function and are trying to figure out how to break the ice and fit in, find a group activity you can be part of. If, for example, the host of the party is asking for volunteers to help serve food or refreshments, pitch in. Not only will you be doing a good deed but you will also have a ready-made excuse to talk to people.

You can also initiate the group activity. Bring a deck of cards with you, and play a game of blackjack or poker with a friend. Chances are, you will draw the attention of others, and before you know it you will have a lively card game going.

Another idea: Bring a fun personality quiz to the event. Read the quiz to a friend as others look on, and pretty soon you may attract a few curious people who want to take the quiz and discuss its implications.

Regardless of the activity, the result will be the same: You will become involved in a group activity that makes it easy for you to start conversations and make friends. And, best of all, you won't have to say a lot to get this going; all it takes is one simple action to bring people together in an atmosphere of fun and enjoyment.

Exercise 6. Helping Hands in Action

In this exercise you will break the ice by helping others.

STEP 1. Before you leave home, meditate on your desire to help people and connect with them. Think of how grateful and open others will be if you offer a helping hand when it's needed.

STEP 2. Wherever you go, be on the lookout for people in need. If you see a frail elderly lady crossing the street, help her cross. You are doing a nice thing, and she might have a son or daughter (or grandson or granddaughter) who may be perfect for you.

Every day make it a practice to give people a helping hand. Offer advice and counsel, help and support. Lend someone a pen, offer directions, help somebody carry groceries. It doesn't have to be anything big; something simple like offering a smile to a tired office worker may be enough to jump-start a conversation and begin a friendship.

STEP 3. Ask for help yourself. Don't be afraid that others won't want to help you; many people are willing to offer a helping hand as long as it's for something small and doesn't pressure or obligate them.

As you go out in the world, focus on doing a few simple humanitarian actions and accepting the kindness offered to you. By doing this you will connect with others in a gracious way, and you will have an excellent opportunity to make new friends.

Reclaim Your Social Space:
Your Romantic Territory

Raised by a perfectionistic mother, Johnny often felt inadequate because he couldn't measure up to her exacting standards. In school Johnny compensated for his feelings of inferiority by excelling in sports and academics. A star player on the tennis team, a 3.8 student, and a leader in student government, Johnny succeeded at almost everything except his personal relationships.

No matter how hard he tried, Johnny alienated others with his seemingly arrogant attitude. The truth was that his act was a cover-up for his intense feelings of shyness and inadequacy. Deep inside Johnny was really a sensitive soul who craved understanding and love.

As a participant in one of my ImprovTherapy groups, Johnny began to turn his social life around by learning how to project an irresistible romantic presence without using a lot of words—by communicating an impressive variety of moods, feelings, and attitudes through his body and facial expressions.

In a short time he was the star of the class. Then one night Johnny shocked the class with four words: "You're a stupid coward!" He was referring to Charlene, one of the newest members of the group—a pretty blond thirty-year-old medical student who was having trouble with one of the exercises. Charlene was supposed to go to the front of the class and verbally take control from Johnny by interrupting his monologue. The problem was that Johnny was still talking, and Charlene was cowering in the back of the room, timidly waiting for just the right moment to interrupt.

"I said you're a coward," continued Johnny. "This is my space, and you're not taking it."

"What?" cried an embarrassed Charlene.

"You're a mousy, shy little bug," replied Johnny. "You don't deserve your own space. Why don't you just crawl into a little corner and hide?"

"Go to hell!" yelled Charlene, as she stormed to the front. "You can't talk to me like that. This is my space, this is my show!"

"Yes, ma'am," replied Johnny with a huge smile as he bowed and left the stage to thunderous applause. Startled at first, Charlene broke into laughter as she realized what had just happened: She had seized her personal space and had finally gotten the respect and attention she deserved.

Later Charlene thanked Johnny, and Johnny admitted he had done it partly because he wanted to get to know her better. "I kind of like you too," mumbled Charlene, as she looked down and lit up like a Christmas tree.

Eight months later, Johnny and Charlene were engaged, and twenty months after that, Charlene delivered their beautiful baby boy, Scott. Now they're hoping Scott turns out to be a shy-sensitive person just like his daddy and mommy so they can teach him all he needs to be happy and successful in the world.

For shy people, social space—the territory of distance, words, and emotions that determines their responses and shapes their self-esteem—is the first frontier. Social space is measured by the degree to which a person is willing to project himself or herself into the social world—how much verbal attention a person is willing to claim, how much physical space he or she is able to occupy comfortably and confidently.

The beauty of social space is that it's entirely flexible, depending on the needs of the situation. Sometimes it's perfectly OK to maintain a small social space, to sit back, listen, and absorb what's being said. At other times a more assertive and expansive sense of space is called for; it's time to speak up, state your case, and express yourself fully.

The problem with many shy people is that they allow themselves to become fixed in a very small social space because they're afraid of looking foolish. Instead of planting their feet firmly on the ground, making direct eye contact, and speaking steadily for significant periods of time, shy people tend to do the opposite: They shift their bodies, engage in flitting eye contact, and speak (assuming they say anything at all) in half sentences, short word clips, or stuttered phrases, weighted down by a meek "I can't believe I'm worth it" voice.

Not only do many shy people get off to a shaky start like this but they also finish weakly. They close the social space too soon—cutting off the interaction before they have a chance to determine whether the other person really likes them. Shy people stop and run because they aren't comfortable and confident enough to extend their social space and take the conversation a step further.

To counteract this tendency, shy people need to create a safe and sufficiently large social space for themselves. They need to stake their claim in the social universe and say: "This is my social space, my emotional territory. Wherever I'm sitting or standing, this is where I belong. Although I may be quiet at times, when I speak I want you to listen to what I have to say."

When you claim your social space, you don't need to raise your voice or act aggressively. You can still be polite, quiet, and sensitive while making the effort to extend the social bubble around yourself—to risk more verbally, emotionally, and physically, to put yourself out more, to get closer to people, in every way possible.

Exercise 7. Become a Space Watcher

If you've been dominated by your critical Observer in the past, chances are you haven't been fully aware of the fascinating way people use space in social situations. Because you've been so focused on yourself, you probably haven't noticed how much impact space can have on social relationships.

According to proxemics, the study of how people use physical space in society, there are four common levels of distance between people:

- *Intimate Distance*: from actual touching to eighteen inches away. This is for those who are emotionally close, such as lovers or dating partners. If you don't move away when someone comes this close, you're probably emotionally connected to that person.
- *Personal Distance*: eighteen inches to four feet. This is for people who feel comfortable together and can be considered friends.
- *Social Distance*: four to twelve feet. This is the polite social distance for people who work together, or for relationships like that between salesperson and customer.
- *Public Distance*: twelve feet and beyond. This is the distance strangers elect to keep. It keeps them detached and in their own private safety zones.

Research shows that shy people prefer to keep more space between themselves and the opposite sex than non-shy people do. While this preference may help shy people feel safer and more protected, it also prevents them from getting emotionally close to others. In this exercise you will learn how to become more observant of space and the way it affects people's emotions and reactions.

STEP 1. Find a partner and stand facing this person, about a foot apart, as both of you look directly into each other's eyes. Notice the feelings you're experiencing as you stand almost face-to-face with this person. You may feel a strong desire to change your body position, either backward or sideways, to avoid being too close to your partner.

STEP 2. Choose a very important character (a king or queen, president, or celebrity) to role-play while your partner chooses a very low-level character (peasant, peon, or dung sweeper).

As the high-status person, you will expand your space and let it flow into your partner's space. If you play the queen, for example, you can stand within several inches of your peon partner as you dangle your arms over your partner's head and exhale in his or her face (hopefully you won't have eaten onions before you do this). Your peon partner will react to your queenly presence by retracting his or her space—kneeling, bowing, and prostrating—as he or she allows you to dominate the space.

STEP 3. Switch roles so you play the low-status person and your partner plays the high one, with corresponding changes in the space dynamic. Take note of any differences in your feelings as you switch from the dominant space user to the submissive one.

STEP 4. Go to coffee bars or other social settings and watch how people use space in social conversations. Find someone who looks like the social leader of a group—the person who talks animatedly and often while holding everyone's attention. Observe how this person uses physical space to project a commanding presence. He or she may bend in close, change body position when making a point, touch people frequently, lean back in the chair, and so forth. Notice how the others react to this person's spatial movements. Do they seem comfortable, interested, intrigued, attracted, or intimidated?

STEP 5. Experiment with space and see what kinds of reactions you can get from others without saying a word. When you walk past someone, for example, pass a little closer than usual and notice his or her reaction. Does the person apologize, emit a nervous laugh, or smile in a friendly way?

As you become more aware of how space is used in social situations, you will begin to see it as a powerful form of communication. You will see the correlation between space and emotional reactions, and you will realize how you have been handicapping yourself by reducing and retracting your space in the presence of others.

Exercise 8. Exploring the Space

In this exercise you will express yourself through space as you leave your mark on the world.

STEP 1. Find a comfortable place where you can work, perhaps your living room, den, backyard, or garage. Recruit a partner.

STEP 2. As you get ready to move through the space you have chosen, imagine that you're going to push through a particular substance that fills the space. Imagine what this substance feels and looks like as you give it a name. If you imagine the substance as a thick, sweet liquid like molasses, you may decide to call it Syrup. If you see it as pure oxygen, you may want to call it O.

STEP 3. Have your partner choose a movement word—*glide, slide, walk, jog, run,* and so forth. He will tell you the word—*glide,* for example—and you will do what he says: You will glide through the substance using your entire body. As you make contact with the substance in your imagination, you will feel it with your mouth, nose, stomach, legs, knees, feet, arms, hands, and every other part of your body. You will experience the substance fully as you explore every inch of the space it fills.

STEP 4. Your friend will keep calling out movement words, and you will react accordingly. You will slide through the substance, you will jump through it, you will jog through it. As you do this, focus on the feelings you're experiencing as you move through the space in different ways.

With this exercise as your guide, you will become more active and creative in your use of space, and you will leave a part of yourself, a trace of your social identity, wherever you go.

Exercise 9. Seizing the Space

How many times have you psychologically crawled into a social situation instead of entering confidently? How many times have you settled for a half-finished good-bye instead of offering others an invitation to get to know you better? If you're shy, you probably have a tendency to make entrances and exits in the social world as if you didn't deserve to be there. Feeling hesitant and anxious, you allow the social space to collapse around you, squashing your self-esteem in the process. Now it's time to reverse this self-defeating trend and learn to confidently and proudly project yourself in social situations. Here's how you do it.

STEP 1. Choose someone to work with, and place that person at the front of the room. Your partner will begin speaking animatedly (swinging his arms, using exaggerated vocal expressions, and so forth) on any topic that strikes his or her fancy.

STEP 2. Leave the room, and enter it again as your partner continues the excited monologue and ignores your presence. When you enter the room, you won't say anything, nor will you do anything that attracts attention to yourself. You will, instead, shrink into the background, avoiding eye contact, slumping, cowering, tiptoeing, doing whatever it takes to be invisible. Mentally record the feelings you experience as you do this.

STEP 3. Now reenter the room in the most attention-grabbing way possible, without saying a word. Come to the front of the room, where your partner is, and decisively take the stage from him or her. Jump, run, do push-ups, make wild facial expressions, take off your shoes and toss them on the floor—do anything else you can think of (other than touching your partner)—to make your presence felt nonverbally. In the meanwhile, your partner will keep trying to ignore you as he or she continues the monologue.

STEP 4. Repeat this exercise, except this time use words to help you seize the space. When you make your grand entrance in Step 3, you can use any verbal expressions you like to grab your partner's attention. You can be angry, sad, funny, charming, playful, or anything else you want to be at that moment.

Try not to yell; your goal is to use your nonverbal presence, not your voice, to make an impact. The most popular person in the room is not necessarily the loudest but the one who knows how to use words and nonverbal expressions to capture people's attention and interest.

VARIATION. Repeat Steps 1 through 4, except this time you will exit the room. Be sure to make an attention-grabbing exit that jolts your partner out of the one-sided monologue and earns you the attention and respect you deserve.

STEP 5. See how much attention and interest you can generate in the outside world simply through the way you position yourself. Clear your throat, brush your hair back, leaf through a magazine, walk next to someone a bit closer than usual, or drop something on the floor.

Another attention-catching approach is to display contrast in your movements and expressions. If the place is noisy, for example, whisper to others. If everyone is walking in a straight line, zigzag around them. If people are sitting down, stand up.

With practice you will detect a definite improvement in your ability to command attention and interest without having to be loud or say a great deal. You will enter and exit a room with elegance and class, and while you're there, others will be drawn to your subtle yet confident nature.

Staying Longer, Feeling Stronger

Shy people have a hard time with the idea of lingering: taking your time in social situations and staying long enough to get comfortable and meet interesting people. Because shy people are afraid of overstaying their welcome and being seen as pushy or inept, they tend to leave social events much too soon and close conversations way too quickly. As a result, they don't give people the opportunity to really get to know them.

A good way to practice the art of lingering is to sit down with a friend and enjoy a relaxed, intimate dinner. Focus on eating patiently, slowly. Savor each bite and relish each and every word spoken. Don't speak too fast; take your time answering questions or responding to comments.

If your Observer is starting to make you feel self-conscious, pause and remind yourself to relax and enjoy each moment. Allow your Actor to come out leisurely and say what needs to be said in the proper time.

Once you have some experience with lingering, try it out in a new social setting. If, aside from being shy, you're also an Introvert, you probably like to go to places early and leave early because your social energy is exhausted pretty rapidly. On this occasion, however, push yourself to linger a bit more. At a dinner party stay until after dessert. At a dance push yourself past midnight. By staying longer you not only gain more social experience, but you also have a better chance of meeting the person you really want to meet.

While you're at the social event, you should also try some lingering conversational moments with a person you're interested in. If you have the urge to leave after a brief exchange, tell yourself that you'll stay a little while longer. You can say a couple of more things or simply sip your drink and stand there quietly for a moment. Who knows? That person may find your quietness intriguing, and he or she may start an interesting conversation with you in the next few moments.

If you give lingering a try, you will find that you're able to meet more interesting people and have a much better time than ever before. By pushing your comfort zone a tad, you will expand your social space and give yourself the opportunity to really shine.

CHAPTER 9

Conversational Romance

"Uh, I, um, work in in re-re-research," sputtered Kelly, a forty-two-year-old biotech research manager as she drowned in the deepest blue eyes she had ever seen. She had just been introduced to Dan, a lethally handsome, forty-three-year-old luxury-car salesman, and her shyness was already getting the best of her.

"You must be a smart lady," replied Dan, with a mischievous grin. She was cute, although a little tense, he thought. Maybe she'd loosen up a bit.

What to say, thought Kelly. Should I say I'm smart—no, that's too vain. Should I laugh it off and say I'm not smart. No, then he'll think I'm dumb. Better to say nothing.

After several moments of silence, Dan tried again: "What do you do for fun?"

Fun? I work all the time, thought Kelly. No, he doesn't want to hear that; he'll think I'm way too boring. What *do* I do for fun?

"Nothing really," answered Kelly, instantly regretting it. How dumb. Now he must really think I'm a dud.

"I'm into hiking, camping, and mountain climbing," said Dan. "I just love the great outdoors. Have you ever gone camping, Kelly?"

Again, Kelly hesitated. If she said yes, she would be lying—she had never been camping. If she said no, she would turn him off because he really liked those things. Knowing she would lose him either way, Kelly fell back into her old pattern of saying nothing, hoping the question would go away and she wouldn't have to answer.

Unfortunately, Dan took her silence as an answer—she didn't like him—and he realized this wasn't going anywhere. He was relieved when a friend said hello and gave him the perfect excuse to leave the conversation. But he was also disappointed; Kelly seemed like a nice and attractive lady. Too bad she had absolutely no interest in him.

Very bad, thought Kelly. She had blown it again. Her dumb mouth had betrayed her for the umpteenth time. She felt like going home and burying her sorrows under a double serving of rocky road ice cream. Dan was so attractive, and she had ruined her chances with him. Why couldn't she say the right things when she met a desirable man?

For many shy people words aren't just words; they're verbal hand grenades, primed to explode in their faces the instant they open their mouths and say the wrong things. As soon as they arrive at a social setting, shy people are visualizing the worst: They imagine themselves clumsily pulling the pins of their verbal grenades and blowing themselves to smithereens. They vividly see the survivors in the room shaking their heads and muttering: "What the hell is wrong with this klutz?"

Of course, shy people don't always come off as socially inept; in fact, they can be quite graceful and conversationally fluent if they feel comfortable in a situation (like when they're hanging out with close friends). As always, the problem lies with the Observer and its relentless promotion of the idea that shy people must be super-charming and extratalkative if they want to win the heart of an ideal person.

When the pressure builds, shy people either clam up (hoping they won't say anything dumb) or spew incoherent sentences in an anxious attempt to say something, anything, just to get the eight-hundred-pound Observer off their backs. To compound the problem, the dating world makes it even more difficult for shy people to achieve their full potential. In today's society many people approach dating in a competitive, do-or-die manner, focusing on how many "points" they can score—how proficient and competent they are at getting phone numbers, dates, sex, companionship, love, and marriage. When shy people fall into this trap, the pressure becomes almost unbearable. Now each word, each sentence, takes on special meaning, added weight. Shy people fret: If I say the wrong words (or if I don't say the right ones), I'll really screw this up. I'll be rejected and abandoned. I'll be single for life.

It doesn't have to be that way. Communicating with an interesting person doesn't have to be torture. Finding a compatible mate is an important and worthy task, but the best way to succeed is by enjoying the process of a conversation (having fun and becoming a better conversationalist), instead of worrying about the product (getting a date or finding a mate).

The Conversational Stroke

Imagine that conversation is like a tennis game. The ball represents the words, and the racket symbolizes each person's unique verbal style. In a conversation one person hits—or strokes—the ball with his or her racket, and the other responds by stroking it back. In ImprovTherapy, a conversational stroke is a complete unit of social communication: a few simple words or phrases that contribute to a conversation and make it easy for the other person to respond. Unlike in tennis, however, the focus is not competitive but cooperative. Instead of scoring points and trying to win, the goal is for two individuals to harmonize and blend their ideas, words, and feelings in a fun, low-pressure way that brings them closer and sets the stage for a possible romantic connection.

The beauty of this approach is that you don't need to worry about impressing a potential mate. All you have to do is offer a few conversational strokes, a few simple words or phrases, that flow naturally and spontaneously in the course of a fun conversation.

A simple but effective stroke interaction can go something like this:

You and that irresistible person (IP) are sitting next to each other at a book signing.

YOU: *Signatures in the Dark* is a great read.

IP: You bet. I want him to sign two copies.

YOU: What did you like about it?

IP: I especially liked the way he wove plot elements from his earlier ones: *Death Dandies* and *Night Lies.* He mixed it up real nice.

YOU: You must read a lot of his books. By the way, I'm Marilyn.

IP: I'm John. Nice to meet you. Do you often come to his book signings?

YOU: Not too often. Can you recommend any of his other books— ones you really enjoyed?

IP: Sure, after the signing, if you want, we can have coffee and talk about it.

YOU: Sounds good.

This stroke-by-stroke approach liberates you from the pressure of having to impress a potential love mate or marriage partner. You can instead kick back and enjoy the process of building an enjoyable and rewarding conversation based on a few brief comments and simple questions about the things that interest you. Conversational strokes should, above all, be enjoyable. Rather than concentrating on results, the successful conversationalist will focus on how much fun he or she can have conversing with an interesting person.

When you're overly focused on romantic results, your energy will be drained because you have artificially created a pain-pleasure, reward-punishment scenario. You think: If I say and do the right things, I will receive pleasure and a reward (a romantic encounter or relationship). If I don't, I will suffer the pain and punishment of romantic failure and loneliness. Now you end up taking every interaction much too seriously and way too personally. If, for example, the other person is having a bad day and doesn't respond well to you, you immediately conclude it's your fault, and your self-confidence takes a big hit.

A much better approach is to let go of your need for results and simply enjoy talking to others in a lighthearted way. To develop this mind-set, ask yourself these questions:

- What is the most fun thing about this person?
- What makes me want to get to know him or her better?
- How can we combine our energies and styles to have a blast together?

Always be on the lookout for ways you can make a conversation more fun—not just for the person you're talking to but for you. It's true: The more fun a conversation is for you, the more fun it will probably be for the person you're talking to.

The One-Stroke Approach to Dating

Fish wasn't the only thing on her mind when Kate, a shy twenty-five-year-old redheaded salesclerk, went shopping at the seafood section of her local grocery store. Actually, there was another kind of catch she was interested in: a twenty-nine-year-old Italian hunk named Lorenzo who had a body that made her feel tingly all over and a sexy, deep voice that soothed her soul. And, yes, he was the guy who sold her seafood, as often as Kate could summon up the nerve to buy it from him.

Although she was a little embarrassed at first, Kate plunged ahead and began interacting with Lorenzo regularly in small ways: smiling, making steady eye contact, and saying hello and good-bye during her seafood shopping sprees. Lorenzo was always polite and friendly toward Kate but didn't appear overly interested in kindling a romance with her.

Not one to give up easily, Kate kept offering a few strokes to Lorenzo each time she saw him. One time she told him about a recipe she was preparing for salmon teriyaki and asked his opinion. On another occasion she mentioned she was going to the opera, and they discussed some classic Italian operas.

Over time Lorenzo began to warm up to Kate, and he started looking forward to their brief conversations. She was always bubbly and interesting, and Lorenzo realized he truly enjoyed her company. "My friend Angelo just opened up a new restaurant," said Lorenzo on one of Kate's visits. "It's supposed to be really good. Would you be interested in going with me?"

"Yes, that would be nice," replied Kate as she rejoiced: Finally! After all these years of shying away from great men and being lonely, I'm going out with the man of my dreams! It's true: Anything is possible, one stroke at a time.

You can be very happy and successful in your romantic life if you use a one-stroke approach to conversation and dating—if you talk to people by using a few simple words or phrases at a time, each building upon the next, until you've created a strong connection.

The key is to take each stroke as far as it needs to be taken, neither overstaying nor understaying your welcome. You want the person you're with to feel relaxed and comfortable, not pressured in any way. The good thing about the one-stroke dating approach is that you can enjoy some minor but satisfying wins as you experience what it's like to have attractive people respond to you in positive ways.

In the course of your day you may, for example, receive a nice smile from a cute stranger, enjoy a brief but thrilling flirtation with a salesclerk, and engage in a couple of fun and friendly exchanges with a new co-worker. As you explore these little pockets of receptivity, you will build up your self-confidence and begin to believe in yourself. You will realize that—contrary to what the Observer has always told you—you're a worthy social being who is capable of being admired and desired by others.

As you practice the one-stroke method, make sure you feel comfortable with the way you're expressing yourself. Give yourself the space and time you need to get in touch with your natural Actor so you can say exactly what you want to say in the way you want to say it.

Exercise 1. Building a Story

Here's a fun exercise to help you perfect the one-stroke approach.

STEP 1. Round up a few friends and ask them to sit on the floor in a circle. Choose someone to start the exercise. This person will say the first word that comes to mind, a word that will be the beginning of a story the group will cocreate. He or she may begin the story with a word like *the, when,* or *how.*

Now the person sitting to the speaker's left will say the first word that comes to mind to continue the story. If, for example, the first speaker said "the," the next speaker may say "politically." Then the next person on the left will add a word, and so on, as everyone in the circle takes a turn contributing to the story, one word at a time. If someone doesn't have a word to add, he or she can say "pass," and the next person will pick up the story.

Keep the story going around the circle, word by word, until you find a natural ending point. Once that point is reached, the next person who speaks will end the story with a final word.

A sample story might go something like this: "The politically correct brown cow ran for president and won because she promised milk for everybody."

STEP 2. Repeat Step 1, except this time each person in the circle will say several phrases or sentences rather than just one word to continue the story. As one individual adds more material, the next person will get ready to jump in and move the story forward. As before, when the story comes to a good ending point, the next speaker will wrap it up.

STEP 3. Immerse yourself in as many one-stroke conversations as possible. Start with basic greetings ("Hello"), compliments ("That looks good on you"), and questions ("What's the best thing to eat in here?"). The key is to offer these conversational tidbits *without expecting anything back.* Don't expect a smile, nice comment, or anything else. You're not doing this to get a good reaction, approval, or a romantic connection; you're doing it only to develop your stroke-giving ability. You're doing it to change your perspective from inner-focused and socially anxious to an outer-focused, fun-loving attitude that helps you connect with others, one word at a time.

You will be like one of those people who gives out free samples at the grocery store. If people like what you have to offer, that's great. If they don't want it, it won't bother you in the least. After all, you have an endless supply of that very valuable commodity known as You.

Offer as Much as They Can Accept

Because shy people are often so worried about being judged, they may not be fully aware of how others are responding to their conversational strokes. For this reason shy people can easily misread a conversational situation: They may offer much more verbal intimacy than others are willing to accept, or far less than others are eager to receive. The best approach is to offer as much information, interest, and intimacy as another person can accept. To accomplish this, shy people need to become more cognizant of how others are responding to them.

Don't make the mistake of allowing your Observer to dissect the situation to death. Instead, use your highly attuned sensitivity to unearth the answers to important questions like these:

- Is my partner ready to accept this conversational stroke right now?
- What kind of conversational flow are we in—a free-flowing, anything-goes moment, or a cautious, wait-and-see vibe?
- As we speak, how do I feel about this person, and how does he or she feel about me?

Here are a couple of exercises to help you become a more sensitive and subtle conversationalist. You will learn how to be aware of the give-and-take nature of conversation while you offer as much of yourself as others are willing to receive.

Exercise 2. The Ball Is in Your Hand

Too many shy people toss out a half-finished conversational stroke and then are disappointed when the other person doesn't respond with strong interest and attraction. A common example is when a shy person asks someone for directions as an indirect way to start a conversation. As a party winds down, a shy individual may say to one of the guests: "Excuse me, can you tell me where the nearest gas station is?" When the gorgeous stranger responds with the requested information, the shy person spits out a too-quick "thank you" and scampers away before the other person has a chance to say anything else. Now the shy person feels disappointed because his or her attempt to start a conversation has ended in a weak thud.

A better, and more complete, follow-up to the helpful stranger's response would have been something like "Thanks. I'm wondering, How do you know the area so well?" With this new and improved stroke, the shy person has offered a clear opening, an opportunity for the other person to continue the conversation if so desired. Now the sexy stranger can return the conversational ball for more conversation or simply let it sail past untouched. Regardless of the decision, the shy person can rest easy with the knowledge that he or she has offered a conversational stroke that is full and complete in its own way.

To help you develop the right mind-set for dispensing conversational strokes, do the following.

STEP 1. Find a small ball (a golf or Ping-Pong ball will work) and a partner. Sit facing your partner, about two feet away, as both of you get comfortable.

STEP 2. Without saying anything, pick up the ball and place it in your partner's outstretched right palm. Your partner will then return the favor by placing it back in your outstretched right palm. Take turns handing the ball to each other silently as you imagine that each transfer represents a conversational stroke, a few playful and spontaneous words or phrases said to a potential romantic partner. Make sure that both of you smile and maintain good eye contact to promote a warm and friendly social atmosphere.

STEP 3. Add conversational strokes to the ball exchange—say whatever comes to mind as you concentrate on your spontaneous Actor. Speak only when you have the ball in your hand. As soon as you place it in your partner's hand, stop talking until your partner says something and hands the ball back to you. Once you have the ball back in your hand, respond with the first thing that comes to mind.

A brief conversational exchange can sound something like this:

> **YOU** (as you place the ball in your partner's hand): You look like you're having a blast.
>
> **YOUR FRIEND** (as he hands the ball back): Yes, and you look like you're ready for takeoff.

IMPORTANT POINT. Don't be overly concerned about being interesting or witty as you hand the ball over. In reality, the exact words don't matter. What does matter is that you give yourself permission to say whatever comes to mind.

STEP 4. In your daily conversations practice handing the ball over to people—saying a few words and then waiting for their response—without expecting anything back. Some people will drop the ball (not respond), while others will put it back in your hand enthusiastically as they signal their desire to continue the conversation and get to know you better.

The beauty of this exercise is that it will help alleviate two common obstacles you may face as a shy person. One problem occurs when you let the ball go too soon (you say too little or speak too fast) because you're afraid of standing out and being judged and rejected. This exercise will help you correct this tendency by showing you how to place the conversational ball in the other person's hand, gently and confidently, as you say what needs to be said.

The other pitfall occurs when you try to hang on to the ball too long, when you talk too much and for too long. Instead of letting go of the ball—offering one conversational stroke and seeing how the other person responds—you try to force your way into your friend's palm with a crush of excess words. You will achieve much better results when you use this exercise to develop a sensitive, give-and-take approach to conversation. With practice you will learn to gracefully and effortlessly dispense conversational strokes based on your natural instincts and on what others are willing to give back to you.

Exercise 3. Dancing Hands

Romantic conversation is like an intimate dance that transforms itself with each new song. Sometimes you and your partner will be in perfect sync, like two professional dancers performing the tango. At other times the dance will be awkward and disjointed as you step on each other's toes and beg to be excused from the dance floor. The best way to succeed in the dating world is to dance conversationally with different kinds of people until you find the person whose style best matches yours. As you do this, always be aware of how others are responding to your conversational moves.

Because of their self-consciousness, shy people may neglect to pick up on the obvious signals from their conversational partner. They fail to recognize whether the other person is really interested in them or whether he or she is just being polite. To avoid this pitfall, you should practice the law of reciprocity: Make sure you carefully balance how much you give—how much energy and interest you offer someone—with how much energy and attention the other person is giving back. At the beginning of a conversation, test the waters by offering a modest conversational stroke. You may ask a simple question, volunteer some personal information, or make a brief comment. The next part is crucial. Watch carefully to see how much the other person gives back. Ask yourself: How much time, attention, and energy is this person willing to contribute to this conversation right now?

If the other person isn't giving back much—if he or she doesn't show much interest by asking questions or speaking in an interested and animated tone of voice—that tells you it's either time to back off and give the person a chance to warm up or time to end the conversation and move on to a more receptive partner.

Here's a good exercise to help you "feel" the conversation and determine the receptivity and interest of your conversational partner.

STEP 1. Find a partner and adopt a sideward stance in which your right foot is leading and both feet are parallel and about shoulder width apart (your partner will stand in the same position). Now slightly twist your head and body so that you face your partner, and raise your right hand at a 90-degree angle (your partner will match your movements). Using the side of your hand, make light contact with your partner's extended right hand.

STEP 2. Push against your partner's hand with slow, steady pressure. Your partner will immediately yield—offering no resistance—as you push your partner's hand back until it touches his or her chest.

STEP 3. Reverse the motion, as your partner does the pushing and you do the retreating until your hand touches your chest.

STEP 4. Continue taking turns pushing and yielding. Your aim is to get to the point where you have a smooth and steady flow, a beautiful harmony of dancing hands.

VARIATION. You can also do this exercise with your eyes closed. It's a marvelous feeling to fully experience (without any visual distractions) the sensitivity that develops around the hands as they naturally flow into each other—back and forth, pushing and yielding, separate yet together.

STEP 5. With your eyes open add conversational strokes to Step 4. The person who pushes back will say a few words—whatever comes to mind—while the other person remains silent. Then the one who was silent will push back as he or she speaks spontaneously while the other listens. Back and forth, each person will take turns pushing and yielding, speaking and listening.

An exchange might go something like this:

YOU (as you push back): Hi, I'm Joanne.

YOUR PARTNER (as he pushes back): Hi, I'm Fred.

YOU (as you push back): Are you free tonight?

YOUR PARTNER (as he pushes back): No.

YOU (as you push back): Are you free *right now*?

YOUR PARTNER (as he pushes back): Yes.

YOU (as you push back): Let's dance.

YOUR PARTNER (as he pushes back): OK, but I lead.

YOU (as you push back): Cool, but only for a moment.

YOUR PARTNER (as he pushes back): No problem. That's the way I like it.

With this exercise as your teacher, you will become more sensitive to the subtle pulls and pushes of the conversational world. You will be more aware of those times when others pull away from you in hesitation and disinterest, and those moments when they push toward you with interest and attraction. Best of all, you will be able to deal successfully with a wide variety of social responses because you understand, and appreciate, the subtle rhythms of human interaction.

To Ask or Not to Ask Questions

What's your name? Do you come here often? What do you do? Where are you from? Ad nauseam, ad infinitum. For some shy people, asking questions is the easy way out but the hard way in. Although questions can be useful as icebreakers and to show interest in someone, shy people often use them excessively to keep the spotlight off themselves. Unfortunately, this interrogating strategy usually backfires. Instead of drawing people closer, asking too many pesky and probing questions pushes them away.

You may not realize how people feel about your question-asking approach. Rather than seeing it as a demonstration of caring and attention, others may perceive it as a sign of selfishness and laziness, as proof that you're not willing to disclose yourself and contribute anything meaningful to the conversation.

To counteract this tendency to overquestion, you first need to become aware of it. Try this.

Find a conversational partner—someone you don't know very well—and begin a get-acquainted conversation as you tape it with a hidden tape recorder (make sure your partner knows he or she is being taped). Later play back the recording and note the number and types of questions you asked and how your friend responded.

Do this again, except this time concentrate on asking as few questions as possible. Simply make statements, and see how you feel (Do you have the urge to ask more questions?) and how your partner responds to your question-light conversational style.

When you interact with others, focus on asking fewer questions and making more statements. This may be hard at first, especially if you've been accustomed to running your conversations through the attention-deflecting route of questions. Yet the more you redirect your questions into statements, the better you will get at it. In time you will become a much more versatile and effective communicator.

Of course, you will still use questions in the right situations. Used properly, questions can be the perfect complements to statements and self-disclosures. Just remind yourself of these important points when you use questions in a conversation:

- *Ask open-ended questions—questions that start with* what, why, *and* how. These questions (What do you like about the concert?) give people the space to maneuver conversationally—to expand on the topic and add new and interesting pieces of information. By contrast, closed-ended questions (Do you like it here?), will unwittingly lock people into boring yes and no answers that stall the conversation instead of moving it along in an intriguing and dynamic manner.
- *Don't ask too many questions.* Timing is important. Asking too many questions in a short time can effectively cut off an interesting conversation. Give your conversational partner the

freedom to answer one question before you pose another. If you hit upon a topic your partner really likes, let him or her keep talking; don't interrupt just to ask a sidetracking question.

- *Keep it personal.* Whether you're asking questions or making statements, avoid the shy person's tendency to tie the conversation around a safe topic like work or school. Talk about yourself instead: your personal interests, hobbies, goals, and feelings. Ask your new friend questions about the same things. Although business and career talk can serve as a good segue to more intimate conversation, too much of it dilutes your romantic power. When it comes to social conversation, always think personal first and business second.

The "Yes and" Approach
to Conversation

Although he didn't realize it, Thomas, a thirty-four-year-old computer programmer, had a self-defeating way of cutting off small talk before it could blossom into something more. On one occasion during work, Jasmine, a cute thirty-five-year-old secretary asked Thomas: "What do you think about astrology?"

"Sorry, I don't follow it," he replied with a shrug. Thomas thought he was just speaking his mind; he didn't realize his curt response was actually cutting off further conversation with a nice lady who wanted to know him better. Thomas wasn't a negative or antisocial person; actually he liked people, and he was usually quite enthusiastic about his interests and hobbies. The real problem was that Thomas had grown up as a shy only child and had never learned the secrets of good communication.

Through a series of self-improvement workshops, Thomas began to upgrade his communication skills and felt ready to make some changes in his social life. Remembering how Jasmine had once asked him a question about astrology, Thomas brought an astrological guide to love and relationships to work. During a coffee break he sat next to Jasmine and began leafing through the book until he caught her eye.

"Do you like astrology?" asked a surprised Jasmine.

"Yes, and I believe you're a Gemini," said Thomas.

"Why?" asked Jasmine.

"Because you seem like you're having double the fun," replied Thomas with the first words that came to mind. Actually, the only astrological sign he knew anything about was Gemini, but he wouldn't mind learning some astrology if Jasmine was his teacher.

Although Thomas was wrong—Jasmine was a Capricorn—it didn't matter. She had always had a crush on Thomas, and now he started to fall in love with her cute shy nature and big brown eyes. Before long, they were dating seriously, and six months later Thomas popped the question.

In the legal world a contract is formed when one party offers detailed terms, the other party accepts, and both parties get something out of the transaction. In the social world a conversational contract is formed when one person makes a conversational offer—puts out a topic for discussion—and the other accepts it by continuing to discuss, and expand upon, the topic with energy and interest. As long as both people get something out of the conversation, it will continue. If one or both parties become bored or restless, the conversational contract will soon be broken, and both people will move on.

Many shy people are not fully aware of romantic conversational offers when they're made, and as a result they miss out on excellent dating opportunities. Like Thomas, shy people can be oblivious to the fact that others want more than a simple exchange of neutral information. Even when shy people become aware of these conversational offers, they often fall back into the defensive position known as *blocking*. Blocking occurs when one person negates or cancels the offer of another, with either an outright no ("Do you know anything about Picasso?" "No") or an indirect one ("How about discussing this over coffee?" "Sorry, I'm too tired; I need to go home").

Even though shy people may want to continue the conversation, they end up blocking it because they're afraid of where it will lead. They're worried they will say something dumb and awkward; they're afraid they will feel pressured and embarrassed by the other person's interest in them. Ironically, the more shy people try to protect themselves with their blocking strategy, the more pain they will feel. Why can't I get close to people? Why don't others like me romantically? These become the inner cries of shy people who don't realize they're stepping on their own toes.

The solution to these social woes lies in acceptance, in being open to the conversational offers made by those around you. In ImprovTherapy terms, this is the "yes and" response. If someone says something to you ("It's a beautiful morning, isn't it?"), you embrace what they say and add something to it ("Yes, and it's going to be even more beautiful tonight"). In this way, instead of negating your partner's conversational offer ("Not really, it's kind of cold"), you accept it, thereby setting the stage for a continuing conversation that is upbeat, lively, and fun.

This doesn't mean, of course, that you have to agree with everything people say. On some points you may have definite opinions and strongly held values. On many others you may not. The truth is that most of us don't have firmly held opinions on a lot of things, and there's quite a bit of room for flexibility in what we choose to say in a lighthearted social conversation.

You can learn a lot by watching talented improvisational actors (stage actors who perform spontaneously, without a script). You will find that they're exceptionally skilled in responding quickly to their fellow actors' words as if they had planned it all out carefully. Their secret lies in their commitment to go with all offers made onstage. If, for example, one of the actors says: "You're the shortest, ugliest person I've ever seen," his or her colleague will respond, "That's right, call me Tiny Terrible."

Of course, unlike a professional improvisational actor, you don't have to accept every conversational offer. You can, however, go a long way toward enjoying social conversations if you become more flexible and adopt the improv actor's "yes and" attitude.

Exercise 4. Blocking and Accepting

This exercise will help you realize what a positive change you can make when you accept instead of block conversational offers.

STEP 1. Find a partner and begin a get-acquainted conversation. Pretend that you have just been introduced at a social function.

You'll make conversational offers—adding new topics and ideas for discussion—and your partner will block the conversation as much as possible, negating what is being offered.

It can go something like this:

> **YOU:** You look kind of familiar. Did you go to USC by any chance?
> **PARTNER:** No.
> **YOU:** Where are you from?
> **PARTNER:** Out of town.
> **YOU:** So now that you're here, what do you like about L.A.?
> **PARTNER:** Nothing.
> **YOU:** The weather is beautiful today, isn't it?
> **PARTNER:** No, it isn't.
> **YOU:** You're pretty negative, aren't you?
> **PARTNER:** No, I'm not.
> **YOU:** Good night.
> **PARTNER:** There's nothing good about it.

STEP 2. Reverse roles. This time your partner will be the one who keeps offering, and you'll be the one who keeps blocking.

STEP 3. Redo Steps 1 and 2, except this time you and your partner will accept everything that's said. You don't have to agree with every detail that is being communicated, but both of you will agree with the spirit of the conversation, which is to move the discussion forward in a friendly and lively way. Here's how it might go this time:

> **YOU:** You look kind of familiar. Did you go to USC, by any chance?
> **PARTNER:** Actually, I went to Arizona State, but maybe we've met somewhere else. It's a small world.
> **YOU:** I agree. Are you originally from Arizona?
> **PARTNER:** That's right, born and bred.
> **YOU:** So now that you're here, what do you like about L.A.?
> **PARTNER:** I love the nightlife.
> **YOU:** Really, what especially?
> **PARTNER:** I'm into salsa dancing. I go every weekend. It's a great time.
> **YOU:** I love salsa dancing too, but I'm just a beginner. Do you know a good place for lessons?

> **PARTNER:** Sure, check out Fandango every Sunday night. They have lessons at eight, dancing at nine.
>
> **YOU:** It sounds like a lot of fun.
>
> **PARTNER:** Actually, I'm going there with some friends this Sunday night. Would you like to meet us there?
>
> **YOU:** Sounds great. I'll be there at eight.

STEP 4. Apply the "yes and" approach whenever you find yourself in social conversations. See how much momentum and positive energy you can generate as you embrace conversational offers and add your own interest and input to the interaction. At the same time, be on the lookout for occasions when you're tempted to halt a conversation. Overall your goal is to be an open and flexible communicator who embraces the ideas and opinions of others and merges them with your own.

The Fun Is About to Begin

You've come a long way in the last few chapters. You've learned how to defeat your pesky nemesis—the Observer—at its own game. You've learned how to warm up your social muscles, get your fools out, and communicate—gracefully and sensitively—with your presence and your words. Along the way you've relieved social pressures, defeated unrealistic romantic expectations, and catapulted yourself into that rare air of social confidence and romantic mastery.

From a social standpoint you've been born again as the Actor: the natural, authentic, and spontaneous part of you that has always been a social winner. This Actor has always known what to do in social situations, has always been sensitive, confident, charismatic, and sexy. All the Actor needed was for you to recognize it, for you to encourage this genius to take center stage in your romantic life.

Now that you've done the hard work—acknowledging and developing your Actor—the rest is easy. Your remaining task is to let your Actor loose and allow it to speak for you. When you place your Actor at the head of your love life, you will be one step closer to attracting and captivating the leading man or lady you've always dreamed about.

PART THREE

The Shy Person's Keys to Finding and Keeping Love

CHAPTER 10

How to Be a
Shy Type Detective

The operation had begun, and Beatriz was alert and ready. In the corner of the room she spied the tall, handsome man with the kind eyes as he drank from an already empty glass—his eyes darting around the room, his feet tapping on the floor like those of a soft-shoe dancer. By the buffet table she saw the gorgeous hunk with the ravishing brunette as he stood about six feet from his companion and made flirty eye contact with several people at the party. And by the entrance she observed the quiet, mysterious-looking man with the swarthy features and sexy-dangerous mustache who stood alone, watching the partygoers with amused interest and making direct, penetrating eye contact with others whenever he felt like it.

After her social investigation, Beatriz realized the good-looking guy with the dancing eyes was probably a shy gentleman who wanted to make a romantic connection but was anxious about doing so. No problem. She liked shy guys, and this one—with his attractive features, tall frame, and gentle eyes—was a definite romantic possibility. Beatriz also concluded that the hunk with the woman was not really *with* her. There was too much emotional and physical space between them. In the past she would have given up immediately as soon as she saw such an attractive couple, but now her eyes told her he was available. Finally, she thought about Mr. Dark and Handsome. He wasn't shy—he had a lot of social self-confidence—and he also seemed comfortable with his own company; he was most likely a non-shy Introvert. She also decided that he was sexy as hell, and that he would make the first move if she signaled her interest with some inviting eye contact.

Tonight Beatriz felt like a romantic Sherlock Holmes. Her mission: to have fun and pick up on all the social clues she could find, on her way to meeting and capturing the heart of Mr. Right. So many clues, so little time, thought Beatriz, as she smiled at Mr. Dark and Handsome and prepared to solve the riddle of this mystery man.

Imagine that you're a private detective who has just been hired by a powerful and influential client. Your mission: To observe people carefully, picking up clues about their habits, behaviors, and personalities to help you identify the One. The One is the person who is interested in developing a romantic relationship with you, compatible with you in every sense of the word, and likely to be your best match in a long-term, fulfilling relationship. Your high-powered client is your Actor, the authentic and natural part of your mind that knows exactly who is best for you. And your nemesis—the one who will try to make your task as difficult as possible—is, no surprise, the Observer.

When you act like a shy type detective, you will become attentive to the simplest of clues. You will observe people to determine their shy types. You will notice the way men and women use subtle (and not-so-subtle) strategies to create rapport with each other. You will observe the clothes people wear to make an impression, the fragrances they use to attract each other. Everywhere you go, you will engage in simple, pure observation.

Although it may seem like a natural thing to do, this kind of observation is not always easy. Because shy people are often so worried about how they're coming across, they're unable to see clearly what others are really like. Rather than focus on how two people are conversing to learn more about them, shy people reflect back on themselves and ask: Do they like me? Rather than study the clothes people wear for clues to their personalities, shy people worry about how they're dressed.

Your goal in this chapter is to become a shy type detective and transform your perspective from inner observation (as controlled by your judgmental Observer) to outer observation (seeing the social world as it really is). You will start by examining something that interests you in the social environment—how people dress, their manner of walking, the way they interact with each other—and continue to explore your interest by asking yourself questions about what you're observing without relating it back to yourself.

Exercise 1. Selfless Involvement: Observe, Wonder, and Perceive
To strengthen your observational skills, try this.

STEP 1. Take a trip in nature—to a park, beach, lake, river, mountain, or desert. Find a comfortable spot, sit quietly, and take a good look around. Focus on experiencing everything in the environment in as much detail as possible: Listen to the singing birds, feel the hot sun, scan the breadth of the sky. Your goal is to become a pure observer, to get outside yourself for a moment, to forget your worries. Stop obsessing about how you're going to pay your taxes or what you're going to do Friday night. Focus, instead, on what you're tasting, touching, seeing, hearing, and smelling, right now. Let your five senses be your guides as you experience everything in the present moment.

STEP 2. Go to a social setting—a party, coffeehouse, or promenade—and observe people. Take a curious attitude with you. Ask yourself as many questions as you can:

- How are the people dressed?
- How do they walk, talk, and position themselves?
- What are their facial expressions and gestures like?
- What do they carry (and not carry)?
- How do they handle objects in their environment?
- How do they react to other people?
- How often do they smile?
- What kind of eye contact do they make?

STEP 3. Make deductions based on your observations. Realize that people often wear their life stories on their faces and express their hidden natures through their gestures, expressions, and vocal quality. For example, you can conclude that the man who covers his mouth when he speaks is nervous and unsure of what he's saying. You may assume that the couple who sit closely, touch each other lovingly, and form a protective cocoon around each other are romantically involved.

The more you do this exercise, the more you will take the focus off you and place it on the outside world. Instead of being tense and worried about failing in a social situation, you will be relaxed, confident, and attentive. You will be like a spectator who is able to enjoy a thrilling sporting event because he knows he's safe in his seat; nothing bad can happen to him there.

Detecting Compatibility:
Finding Your Ideal Shy Type

It took Charlie, a shy Introverted thirty-five-year-old mechanic, fifteen years of dating before he realized why he had never been in a satisfying, long-term love relationship. Charlie kept getting involved with his exact opposite: outgoing, take-charge, Extraverted women who wanted to dominate him.

Of course, things were often kind of nice in the beginning: Charlie enjoyed laying back and letting the Extraverted woman take the initiative, while she was soothed by Charlie's quiet, easygoing nature. But once the honeymoon period was over, things would take a 180-degree turn for the worse. Charlie's Extraverted partner would start attacking him for being so quiet and unassertive: "Why don't you go out with me and our friends instead of staying home like a couch potato? Why don't you take charge more often? What are you, a man or a mutt?"

Finally, Charlie's next-door neighbor introduced him to a Christian dating service that classified its members by social type. To make sure he didn't repeat the same mistake, this time Charlie focused on meeting a nice, shy, Introverted lady who also had good religious and moral values.

He found his shy, Introverted sweetheart in Kirsten, a gentle, twenty-seven-year-old divorced mom of two who loved baking, church volunteer work, and taking care of her family. Unlike his previous partners, Kirsten was perfectly happy staying home with Charlie, watching videos, cuddling by the fireplace, and reading the Bible. They were a match made in heaven, and they were grateful God had brought two shy Introverts like them together to share a lifetime of happiness.

Many shy people lie awake at night wondering if they will ever find the right partner. Wrestling with loneliness and frustration, they ask: Is there one person out there who is just right for me? If so, where is this person, and why can't I find him or her?

The good news is that there is not just one person for you; there are actually a number of people in the world who could meet your romantic criteria. But before you can meet an ideal person, you first need to recognize him or her as a compatible match, as someone who will be a natural fit with your shy type (the one you determined in Chapter 4 with the Shy Type Quiz).

Your shy type is crucial because it can affect so many important issues, including how satisfied you will be with your mate, where you will live, what type of sex life you will prefer, how many children you will want, what kinds of activities you will enjoy, and what type of social and family circle you will maintain. Once you've recognized and embraced your own shy type, your next step is to look outward and identify the person who is most likely to be compatible with you in a long-term relationship.

Here are research-based relationship recommendations for your shy type, as well as pointers on how to recognize the right shy type for you.

Caveat: The shy type combinations detailed here are only recommendations. You may be able to develop a perfectly satisfying and harmonious relationship with someone who doesn't fit into one of these combinations, although your chances are probably better with the recommended matches.

Shy Introverts

Shy Introverts have the inward-flowing energy (and the privacy needs) of the Introvert and happen to be shy on top of that. Their shyness can make them sensitive and self-reflective in social settings and fearful of being judged and criticized by important and attractive people.

Male shy Introverts are most compatible with shy Introvert partners. Female shy Introverts are most compatible with shy Introvert, non-shy Introvert, and shy Extravert partners (as long as they're not strongly Extraverted; that is, they scored only a 4 or 5 on Extraversion).

Shy Introverts may blush, hesitate, and stammer when they speak.

Their eyes will dart and avoid yours. If they have a drink, they may keep drinking nervously even though there's nothing in the glass. If they decide to dance (which they may be reluctant to do), they may rush out onto the dance floor and avoid eye contact.

Shy Introverts usually want a lot of physical space between themselves and people they don't know very well. At social events they may sit in a quiet, secluded corner of the room. If they speak at all, they may talk in short, quick bursts or wordy, drawn-out sentences. They may ask a lot of trivial questions just to keep the focus off themselves. They may frequently fold and unfold their hands. A shy man may run his fingers over his beard or balding head to seek reassurance. A shy woman may cling to her purse or other possessions to gain a sense of stability.

Shy Introverts are often alone and seem comfortable with their own company. You may see them dining alone while reading a book or newspaper, or catch them watching a movie by themselves. If you look into their eyes, you may notice a somewhat dreamy or detached look. Because they value their inner life so much, they can retreat into their own thoughts and imaginations easily, regardless of what's going on in the real world. They tend to hang out with only a few close friends and acquaintances, maintaining long-term relationships with a handful of special people. When they're not with close friends, Shy Introverts like to spend a lot of time at home reading, writing, thinking, meditating, listening to music, watching videos, surfing the Net, or tinkering around the house.

Non-Shy Introverts

Non-shy Introverts get most of their energy from their own thoughts and like to spend a lot of quality time by themselves or with a few close friends in private, quiet, and relaxed settings. Because they're not shy, they usually don't have the heightened sensitivity and self-reflection that are characteristic of shy people.

Male non-shy Introverts are most compatible with shy Introvert and non-shy Introvert partners. Female non-shy Introverts are most compatible with non-shy Introvert, shy Extravert, and non-shy Extravert partners (as long as they're not strongly Extraverted; that is, they scored only a 4 or 5 on Extraversion).

When non-shy Introverts go to social events, they like to go early and leave early. While they're in social situations, they can be quite entertaining and charming for short periods—quick and intense bursts—until their energy runs out and they need to go home to recharge their batteries. As deep thinkers, non-shy Introverts may not give you an immediate answer when you ask them something. They usually want to mull things over, and perhaps write their ideas down, before they come to a definite conclusion and communicate their thoughts to you.

Shy Extraverts

Shy Extraverts share the sensitivity and reflection of shy Introverts but have a different way of getting energized: They like to get energy from other people and by socializing in the outside world.

Male shy Extraverts are most compatible with Shy Introvert, non-shy Introvert, and shy Extravert; (as long as they're not strongly Extraverted; that is, they scored only a 4 or 5 on Extraversion). Female shy Extraverts are most compatible with shy Extravert and non-shy Extravert partners.

Shy Extraverts tend to have quite a few friends and acquaintances. They usually like to leave a party or social event late, and they get more energy as the night progresses. They may be quiet at the beginning of a social event (especially when their shyness is active), but once they warm up—especially if they're around familiar people—they can really bust loose and express their Extraverted side. They like to have friends over on a regular basis. They also like to visit their friends and do fun, social things, like going out to concerts, nightclubs, comedy clubs, and parties.

Shy Extraverts like to spend time in the outside world, even when they're not talking to anyone. A shy Extravert, for example, may be too shy to speak with anyone at a coffee shop, but she'll spend a lot of time there anyway: studying, reading, or just people watching. She likes the external stimulation—observing people, listening to them talk—regardless of whether she says anything to them.

Non-Shy Extraverts

Non-shy Extraverts are the outgoing, sociable types who have a wide circle of friends and tend to get energy from other people. They also have relatively thick skins in social situations and don't suffer from excessive self-consciousness.

Male non-shy Extraverts are most compatible with non-shy Introvert, shy Extravert, and non-shy Extravert partners (as long as they're not strongly Extraverted; that is, they scored only a 4 or 5 on Extraversion). Female non-shy Extraverts are most compatible with non-shy Extravert partners.

Non-shy Extraverts—especially those who score high on the Extravert scale of the Shy Type Quiz (6 or 7)—are often the life of the conversation or party, and they love it that way. Their Rolodexes are full, their social schedules are jammed, and their social and romantic lives are usually overbooked. They tend to have a lot of friends and acquaintances. They are well-known and well-connected in the outside world: They know the best plumbers, the smartest CPAs, the most entertaining parties, and the tastiest sushi restaurants. They're the ones you may see at the center of the dance floor, or up on the stage, boogying the night away. They like to tell stories and jokes, and they love to make people laugh.

Non-shy Extraverts maintain steady eye contact and like to smile and laugh often. They typically dress in the latest fashions and use clothes to convey a clear message to others: "I'm friendly. Come and meet me."

WHY CERTAIN SHY TYPES GO BETTER TOGETHER

As you may have noticed, there are gender differences in each of the compatibility recommendations; for example, the best match for a male non-shy Introvert is not the same as the best match for a female non-shy Introvert. These differences are based on research in personality types, gender, and relationship satisfaction.

One important finding, which I mentioned in my last book, *LoveTypes*, concerns the problems Introvert men tend to have with Extravert women in relationships. Male Introverts who are paired with female Extraverts tend to have more problems than any other Introvert-Extravert combinations when it comes to friends, chores, interests, recreation, communication, and sex.

Part of the problem is in the way men and women have been socialized in intimate relationships. Even though society is changing, men have traditionally been taught to be the outspoken and assertive ones in relationships, while women have been encouraged to be the listeners and followers. As a result, Introvert men who have been raised in the traditional way may feel overwhelmed and intimidated by strong-minded, outspoken Extravert women. Likewise, their Extraverted female partners may mistakenly interpret their Introvert men's quiet and laid-back natures as indicating weakness and behavior that is not representative of real men.

Aside from the Introvert-Extravert issue, my research indicates that, overall, shy-sensitive people tend to do better in relationships with other shy-sensitive individuals. If you think about this, it makes sense: Shy people, with their sensitive, reflective natures and desire for quietness, warmth, intimacy, and privacy, are naturally suited for each other. Their similarities make it easy for them to create close and loving relationships.

Detecting Interest:
Finding the Fish That Bites

For most of his adult life, Ralph, a shy, good-looking thirty-two-year-old software designer, had stumbled through the dating world with blinders on. Because Ralph was usually self-conscious in the presence of attractive women, he often failed to recognize when a woman was actually interested in him. He would avoid eye contact and neglect to pick up on the subtle signals that would tell him she was interested in more than just small talk.

Fortunately, one of his successfully shy friends, Jim, recognized Ralph's problem and offered to help. Jim gave Ralph pointers on how to read a woman's body language to determine her romantic interest. Intrigued by the idea of using body language to improve his dating results, Ralph read several books on the subject and began applying his newfound knowledge to his own conversations with women.

At the last big party he attended, Ralph recognized all the "go" signals immediately from Latasha, a pretty forty-two-year-old African American dentist with an hourglass figure and contagious laugh. Everything she did—playing with her hair, caressing her drink, giving him undivided eye contact (with enlarged pupils), and ignoring a couple of men who wanted to talk to her—pointed to one fantastic, obvious conclusion: She wanted to know him much better.

Ralph felt the same way, and this time he didn't miss his opportunity. After discovering they both loved R&B music, he invited her to a Luther Vandross concert the following weekend. Soon they were dating steadily, on their way to a blazing love affair that continues to light up their lives with fun, passion, and nonstop love.

Imagine if you could take all the guesswork out of dating, if you could tell immediately whether someone was interested in you by picking up on certain clues—the way a person looked at you, spoke to you, and dealt with objects and physical space in your presence. Would that make dating easier? Would that increase your odds of meeting the right person and developing a lasting relationship with him or her? Chances are, it would.

If you were absolutely sure that someone was interested in you—and you were equally interested in him or her—you might pursue that person more than usual, and you would probably have a better than average chance of making a romantic connection. Unfortunately, it's not always so easy, especially if you're shy. First of all, the more self-conscious you are as a shy person, the less likely you are to pick up on clues that someone is romantically interested in you. When you're petrified of being judged and rejected by an attractive person, even obvious signs of romantic interest—the cute person is offering you a home phone number, fax number, and E-mail address although you didn't request them—don't make much of an impression on you.

Even worse, you misread neutral signs as indicating a lack of interest. If, for example, she excuses herself to go to the bathroom, you automatically interpret it as meaning she's dumping you (what if she really has to go?). If he looks at his watch, you immediately think he's bored with your conversation (it might also mean he's running late for his flight).

Because you're so used to the Observer's attacks on your social and romantic worthiness, you tend to jump to self-defeating conclusions based on scant evidence. You think: This gorgeous person doesn't like me; I'm not good enough for that honey pie. As if that weren't bad enough, you give up too soon and close the conversation before you really have a chance to get acquainted with that interesting person.

Fortunately, things look a lot better when you play the shy type detective game. Instead of focusing on your personal failings and inadequacies, you will be much more interested in finding out what people are really like. Now when you see a man enter a room with a woman, you won't automatically assume they're lovers and give up on the possibility of meeting the one you're interested in. You will consider other possibilities: Are they friends, siblings, or co-workers? To find out for sure, you'll observe them closely. Do they hold hands, kiss, and give each other undivided attention? If so, they're probably a tight couple. Or do they seem to ignore each other for long stretches of time and talk to others in a flirtatious manner? If so, they may be open to dating new people.

With your new mind-set, you will realize that many of your previous assumptions about people weren't very accurate. In fact, your tendency to assume the worst has undoubtedly cost you romantic opportunities and prevented you from knowing what it feels like to be truly desired by an attractive person.

Although a sexy person may have been crazy about you in the past, you blocked his or her interest out of your mind because it felt too awkward, scary, or simply different. You were so used to putting yourself down that it was hard for you to imagine that such an incredible person could be interested in little old you. Yet, regardless of how old you are, and how many times you've been frustrated and confused, things will be much different when you become a shy type detective. Instead of seeing social situations with uncertainty, you'll perceive them more realistically as you accurately gauge who's romantically interested in you and who isn't.

As you go out into the social world and sift through all the potential dating candidates, you should always keep this advice in mind:

WHEN IT COMES TO CHOOSING A DATING PARTNER, ALWAYS GO FOR RED HOT—NEVER SETTLE FOR LUKEWARM.

Instead of wasting time on people who are lukewarm or neutral toward you, focus on those few special individuals who demonstrate strong romantic interest from the very beginning. Don't wait for chemistry to develop; see how much is already there right now.

Of course, most people will give you signals of romantic indifference when you first meet them. They may not know you well enough to be attracted to you, or maybe you're just not their type. That's OK. What really matters is that you begin to recognize those few occasions when you feel the romantic attraction coming from someone almost instantly. You may feel it during the first few conversational exchanges, or even during the first few words or glances. You will notice the way his pupils expand when he talks with you, the way she touches and grooms herself as she speaks, the way he asks you personal questions, laughs at your jokes, and generally makes you feel important and valued.

No, you may not fall in love with this person and marry him or her. But you can definitely learn a great deal—and raise your confidence and self-esteem in the process—by knowing that you're worthy of someone's romantic interest and attraction.

Of course, you will be careful not to lead this person on if you're not interested in a romance. No matter what happens, you will still be exceptionally respectful and kind to this person. At the same time, you will explore what it feels like to be admired and desired, and you will graciously receive the warmth and attraction this person is offering. Who knows? You may become attracted to this person over time. You may even fall in love. But that's not the important point here. The key is for you to experience that marvelous feeling of knowing that someone really wants to get to know you in a romantic way.

Eventually, you will be so good at detecting this feeling that you will be able to apply your skills when you're really attracted to someone. When the stakes are higher and the pressure is greater, you will have the confidence and clarity of mind to determine whether that gorgeous person actually has a romantic interest in you.

The ability to detect romantic interest is especially important for shy people because they spend so much time in their lofty imaginations. Often a shy person will harbor a secret crush on someone who doesn't even know he or she exists. The shy person may keep up this fantasy life for a long time and consequently waste an incredible amount of time and energy.

Why do some shy people mentally pursue people who are not really interested in them? Or worse, why do they stay in relationships with people who don't cherish them? The answer is that, deep down, many shy people don't believe they deserve to be loved. They genuinely think they aren't good enough to be with a compatible partner who truly cares about them. If you're one of those shy people who is still wasting time mentally chasing people who are no good for you, think about this: Every moment you spend chasing the wrong person is one more wasted opportunity to meet your dream mate.

The Signs of Romantic Interest

To get in the right frame of mind to detect someone's romantic interest, ask yourself the following questions:

- What does this person's body language tell me about his or her interest in me? Is this person friendly, neutral, or uninterested?
- Does this person seem genuinely interested in getting to know me, or is he or she just making polite conversation?

- How much is this person willing to sacrifice—in time, money, other people, activities—just to be with me?
- How many questions (and what kinds) does he or she ask to indicate interest in me?
- Does this person's eye contact indicate that he or she is focused on me and attentive, or does it tell me he or she is uninterested?

In addition to these questions, keep the following checklist in mind to help you determine someone's romantic interest in you.

Displays Romantic Interest	Neutral or Uninterested
Is alert, energetic	Is tense, restless
Has dilated pupils	Has normal or small pupils
Opens posture gradually	Maintains closed posture
Lowers drink	Keeps drink chest-high
Touches self gently	Grips or pinches self
Caresses objects in environment	Squeezes, taps objects
Crosses legs, keeps them steady	Swings crossed legs
Touches you for any reason	Never touches you
Loosens anything	Tightens anything
Leans forward	Leans away
Has steady hands, feet	Taps and drums hands and feet
Provides undivided attention	Is distracted, looking around
Blows friends off for you	Considers friends more important
Returns phone calls quickly	Takes a lot of time to return calls; others always answer the phone when you call
Talks about things both of you can do in the future	Doesn't mention future plans that include you
Shows a strong interest in your life; asks lots of personal questions	Doesn't ask questions about you
Changes something about his or her appearance to please you	Changes nothing
Laughs hard at your jokes	Doesn't laugh
Is available	Is always busy

Exercise 2. Become a Dating Detective

It's time now to put your shy type detective skills to good use.

STEP 1. Read some books on body language (try *Secrets of Sexual Body Language* by Martin Lloyd-Elliot, and *Body Language* by Julius Fast), and write down the signals for romantic availability and interest. Incorporate the questions and tips from the previous two sections (detecting compatibility and detecting interest) into this list until you have created a master shy type detective checklist that contains all the things you need to know to read potential romantic partners accurately.

STEP 2. Go out and practice your shy type detective skills as a neutral observer first. Watch people in social settings and determine their shy types. See if you can tell which people are romantically interested in each other. Based on your observations, for example, you may conclude that the person sitting by himself, carefully nursing a drink and shrewdly checking out the room, is a non-shy Introvert. You may also decide that the man and woman by the bar are a serious couple based on the way they gaze into each other's eyes and position themselves to shut out the rest of the crowd.

STEP 3. Apply your detective skills to your own social life. When you see someone who strikes your fancy, observe him or her carefully. See if you can determine the individual's shy type. If you get an opportunity to talk with this person, clear your mind of the Observer, and focus on picking up romantic signals: Is this person interested in me? If so, how much?

Finally, if you should happen to strike up a friendship or romance with this person, make sure you confirm your earlier assumptions. Give your friend the Shy Type Quiz, and see if his or her score matches your earlier judgment. Also, ask your friend if he or she felt any romantic attraction toward you when you first met.

From Shy Type Detective to Real-World Romantic Expert

You've now taken the crucial first steps toward succeeding in the dating world as a shy person: You've learned how to be a shy type detective who can determine the romantic interest and compatibility of anyone you meet in a social situation. As a bonus, you've begun to turn the tables on the Observer. Whereas before you were consumed by the Observer and its preoccupation with people observing and judging you, now you can relax and become an objective observer. You will be the one who observes others and analyzes social situations in a clear and levelheaded way; you will be the one who makes intelligent judgments about people. As you start looking at others instead of yourself, your Observer will begin to evaporate, and your outward-looking Actor will take over.

With your Actor in charge, not only will you see social situations more realistically—pinpointing those people who are the best romantic candidates for you—but you will also be far more confident about your social worthiness. As you move the focus away from yourself and toward others, you will realize a powerful truth:

NO ONE IS PERFECT; EVERYONE HAS FLAWS AND IMPERFECTIONS. ALTHOUGH YOU MAY BE IMPERFECT AS WELL, YOU'RE JUST AS VALUABLE AND WORTHY OF LOVE AS ANYONE ELSE.

With this new realization, you can loosen up and stop worrying about whether you're good enough to win the love of an ideal person. You are more than good enough—you're a shy-sensitive person who can offer the world to the right partner.

CHAPTER 11

Winning Dating Strategies for the Shy-Sensitive Person

The weekend was here, and Oscar, a timid twenty-three-year-old electrician, looked to his "bible"—*Real Man Dating: 101 Ways to Snag a Babe*—for dating inspiration. Oscar knew he was a nice guy and had a lot to offer, but women just didn't seem to like nice guys anymore; they wanted the macho brutes. That was why he was learning the Real Man approach.

"Say, sweet honey, can I buy you a drink?" asked Oscar as he practiced Real Man Way number 89 in front of his mirror at home. "The same to you," said Oscar with an affected sarcastic voice as he perfected comeback response number 89a in case the woman rejected number 89. Satisfied that he was ready to hit the scene, Oscar drove to one of the most popular beach bars in the area.

As soon as he arrived, however, Oscar started feeling uncomfortable. It happened every time; he was so pumped up when he left the house, but when he got to the crowded, noisy bar full of great-looking people, his confidence vanished and he found himself struggling for words. Still, it was Friday night, and he had to try some Real Man ways. Nervously approaching the first blond woman he saw sitting alone at the bar, Oscar blurted out: "Buy you a drink, sweet honey?"

"Sure, why not?" replied Harry, the blond, long-haired surfer, as he turned around and faced Oscar. "Do I know you?" Embarrassed beyond belief, Oscar raced toward the exit, stomping on a few feet as he went.

"Watch it, jerk!" yelled one of the stepped-on customers as Oscar made a hasty, humiliated departure.

Once he got home, Oscar pulled out his dating bible and looked for words of wisdom to soothe this damaged soul. He found these familiar and comforting nuggets of wisdom: "*Rejection* is just a nine-letter word. Go back and try it again. Never quit. Never say never."

Slowly Oscar built up his resolve again with the advice from his Real Man dating program. I'll keep trying until I get this right. Next time I'll be prepared, and I'll succeed. I'm a real man, yes I am.

When it comes to dating, many shy people are confused. They have so many questions but so few satisfying answers. Should I go out more—to parties, nightclubs, and bars—to meet more eligible singles? Should I be more assertive in trying to find a special someone, or should I stop looking and trust in the principle that you find what you're looking for when you're not looking? Should I use personal ads, Internet dating, or join a dating service to meet Mr. or Ms. Right? Or should I just give up on the whole dating jungle and become a monk or nun?

To make matters worse, many of the dating books, seminars, and tapes out there offer advice that's in direct opposition to shy people's sensitive and self-reflective natures. Shy people are told to get over their shyness and go out more, to do things that not only make them feel uncomfortable but violate the essence of their shy-sensitive personalities.

In this chapter you will find something different: You will learn field-proven tips, techniques, and strategies uniquely tailored to your shy-sensitive needs, concerns, and attributes. The advice here will be exactly what you need to help you overcome any self-imposed obstacles so you can gradually earn your comfortable and rightful place in the shy-dating world.

Altruism as a Dating Strategy: Being Kind Is Sexy

"Being kind is sexy; being compassionate is irresistible." These were the words of advice I gave Majid, a sad-eyed forty-four-year-old claims adjuster, on one of his visits to my office for shyness coaching. Never married, desperate for a wife and especially children, this kindhearted but lonely man was in a very tough place in his life. I knew there was hope for Majid because this gentle, sensitive man had a lot of love to give the right woman. All he needed was a new strategy that would accentuate his strengths—caring, giving, and compassion—to help him find the love of his life.

Majid started with simple things he had always wanted to do but felt too embarrassed to try: smiling and saying hi to strangers who walked by, holding doors open for people, helping a lady carry her bags. His self-consciousness began to evaporate as he started enjoying himself and realizing how easily he could connect with others.

"What do I do now, Dr. Avila?" asked a much more confident Majid. "I feel I can do much more."

"One word," I replied. "Volunteer. Find something you really love to do and give your gift to others."

"I love to play the accordion—polkas, ballads, everything," said Majid. "And I sing OK too. I think I'd like to help the elderly by playing and singing for them."

With this statement as his mission plan, Majid started volunteering his musical services at various nursing homes in his community. He would play his accordion and encourage the residents to sing along. Everywhere he went he got a great response and felt grateful for the opportunity to be of service.

On one occasion Adriana, an attractive brunette of forty, came up to Majid with tears in her eyes, and said: "You've meant so much to my father tonight. Thank you so much. If you're free afterward, I'd like to talk to you some more about the wonderful work you're doing. I think it's great."

Majid took Adriana up on her offer and soon discovered they had a lot in common: Both had been only children, had lost parents to Alzheimer's, and loved music, children, and animals. They agreed to see each other again and before long started dating seriously. Now they're planning to get married and start a small family in the next couple of years. They're also planning to open a nonprofit foundation that sends musicians and comedians out all over the United States to entertain and inspire the elderly. With their hearts for volunteering, there is no limit to the good work they can do in the world, and no limit to the love they can share with each other and their soon-to-be family.

Yes, it's true: Being kind is sexy, being compassionate is irresistible.

If shy people worldwide would embrace and fully live according to this premise, there would no longer be a need for shyness and dating books, shyness therapists, dating courses, matchmakers, and the like. Sure, people would still be shy, but they wouldn't be lonely or frustrated or self-conscious anymore. They would be happy, loving, and free human beings who would be able to connect with each other easily from their Actor's instincts.

It's not difficult to see why: When you focus on giving yourself to others—sharing your time, energy, and love—you won't be able to devote so much attention and energy to your personal inadequacies. No matter how hard you try, it's impossible to have two mental states at the same time. Either you're wrapped up in your own precious preoccupations—worried about your social performance, obsessed with how you're coming across to others—or you're outside yourself, concerned about others and how they're doing, interested only in helping and caring for them.

Every time you offer someone a smile, a nice hello, or a compliment, you're moving a little further away from your self-conscious Observer. Every time you help someone with a task or give advice, you're expanding your Actor. Every time you volunteer for a charity, nonprofit foundation, or good cause, you're doing far more than helping others—you're expanding your view of the social world so that it incorporates more than just you, it includes the entire world and everyone in it.

By contrast, when you allow the Observer to make you self-conscious and fearful, you have no love to give, no kindness to offer. The more you turn your focus inward, the more you isolate yourself from others and see yourself as desperate, frustrated, and lonely. If you give no love, you receive no love; it's as simple as that.

The secret to social happiness, therefore, is to reverse your focus from inward to outward, from the Observer to the Actor, from you to them. If you want to be loved, be loving. If you want to receive attention and affection, offer the same. If you want to be a confident and successful master of the social universe, make other people feel at ease, make them feel valued and wanted. Find shy, Introverted people who look out of place and help them: talk to them, give them compliments, introduce them to people. Take care of their social and practical needs. Ask yourself this question every time you meet a new person: How can I make this person's life a little bit easier and better? Can I offer this person my chair? Give him some advice? Share my cab?

Don't worry about whether the other person will accept what you have to offer. Some will, some won't. Don't be concerned that you will get something out of the interaction; sometimes you will, sometimes you won't. What really matters is that you're transforming your perspective on human relations. You're developing love and compassion as a daily habit, as an integral part of your life. When you think only of what you can offer others, instead of what you can get, the results will amaze you.

First of all, your self-esteem will skyrocket. In the past you may not have felt you were worthy enough to be in a serious relationship; you may have thought you were somehow fatally flawed because you were shy. Now, as you start doing good things for other people, you will create an entirely new view of yourself. You will regard your sensitivity as a great talent. You will see yourself as a valuable member of society because you're doing something that few people are willing to do: offering your sensitivity, compassion, and good works to benefit the world, one person at a time.

Your attitude toward dating will also change. Whereas before you may have been primarily concerned with getting phone numbers, dates, and relationships, now you will be interested only in helping people and making their experience with you as pleasurable and beneficial as possible. When you focus on offering benefits to others, your self-consciousness will diminish, and you will enjoy social interactions a whole lot more. Because you're concentrating on the other person, you won't give the Observer the opportunity to neuter your effectiveness by making you feel nervous and self-conscious. You will instead be relaxed, free-flowing, and at your most impressive, precisely because you're not trying to impress; you're interested only in giving.

Get started by volunteering for an altruistic or charitable organization that helps people in a significant way. When you get involved in such a program, you will be working with like-minded people to make a difference, and your self-esteem and social skills will grow considerably.

There are many reputable charitable organizations that need your help. Look them up in the yellow pages or the *Encyclopedia of Associations* (available at your local library); search the Internet; or contact your local church, synagogue, temple, mosque, or chamber of commerce.

Here are a few ideas to get you started:

- Join a literacy group that helps people learn how to read.
- Volunteer at a local humane society.
- Work at an Alzheimer's clinic.
- Be part of an organization that takes inner-city kids on weekend excursions to the country.
- Join a group that visits elderly residents at retirement homes or cheers up sick children in hospitals.
- Join an organization that provides support and classes for abused and battered women.
- Join a group that strives to save the environment.
- Deliver food and services to shut-ins.
- Work for a counseling or suicide hot line.
- Get involved in one of the ministries at your local church or synagogue.
- Join some friends and help raise money for worthy causes—like AIDS, world peace, and cancer—by participating in telethons, marathons, carnivals, and the like.

When you do good deeds and work for humanitarian causes like these, you're not just doing a tremendous service for humanity, you're also doing a great service for your dating life. It's true: Altruism is good romance. By working in a charitable organization, you will have a great opportunity to meet caring people in a positive, helping setting. If you meet someone you like, you will have the chance to get to know that person in a deep and meaningful way because you will be working as a team to accomplish a worthy goal. Even if you never meet anyone at these volunteer activities—which, of course, you will—you will still receive many great rewards by being a true humanitarian. Just think of that lovely smile from a disadvantaged child you helped, the heartfelt thank-you from a senior at a rest home, or the wet lick from a grateful puppy whose life you have saved. These are the intangible, real-world rewards you receive when you help others.

Dating Strategies for the Shy Person

Dating is different for shy people. What works for others may not work for you because of your special needs. Here are some field-tested dating tips that will appeal to your shy-sensitive nature and help you find your ideal mate.

Dating Courses, Tapes, and Books:
What Works, What Doesn't

It's unfortunate that many shy people spend a great deal of time and money on dating courses, tapes, and books without getting much in return. Some dating courses, for example, tell you to match and mirror others' responses—to breathe and act exactly like they do—so you can win their affections. Other approaches tell you to seduce people with the tone of your voice. Some experts tell you to play it cool: Don't give too much information too fast, don't return phone calls, play hard to get. Still others advise you to be aggressive: approach people in supermarkets and Laundromats, and while standing in line; hit the nightclub and singles circuit; go out on as many dates as you can.

The underlying premise of most of these approaches is that you need to change yourself to attract someone and win his or her heart.

What they don't tell you is that if you have to change yourself to impress other people, you will always be changing yourself; you will never be comfortably you.

When you try to be something you're not, you take all the joy out of dating. After all, dating should be easy; romance should be fun. If it takes to much effort, it's not fun. It's drudgery. Why don't you try something different? Why don't you try being yourself at all times and see what happens? When your Actor is in charge, you don't have to try to be clever or manipulative to win someone over; you can simply be yourself and attract your ideal partner with your innate charm, goodwill, and sensitivity.

To increase your dating effectiveness, you should share your shy-sensitive talents only with those people, and in those environments, where you feel truly valued and appreciated. If, for example, you enjoy reading, you may want to join a literacy organization. If cooking is your thing, you can join a group that brings home-cooked meals to shut-ins and others who can't cook for themselves. As you volunteer your talents, you will meet like-minded people who appreciate your giving and sensitive nature and want to connect with you in the deepest way possible.

The beauty of this approach is that you will naturally attract those special people who are perfectly compatible with you just the way you are. These are your people, the ones who fit you like a glove. You don't need to change for them; *you are already what they want.*

How Do I Break the Ice as a Shy Person?

For many shy people, it's the beginning—saying hello and breaking the ice—that's the hardest. Fortunately, there are plenty of good icebreaking ideas that can work for you, depending on your level of shyness and willingness to take a risk. Some shy people, for example, are willing to talk to strangers in certain situations; others feel comfortable only speaking with people they've known for a while.

When it comes to icebreakers, the best advice is to tailor them to your comfort level. Read some popular books on icebreakers (try *Fifty Ways to Find a Lover: Proven Techniques for Finding Someone Special* by Sharyn Wolf), and try the strategies out in your dating life. If you put your mind to it, there is no limit to the number of fun, shy-comfortable things you can do to break the ice and meet interesting people.

Consider these possibilities:

- Write an intriguing mystery note to someone you like. Cut the note in half and on the top half write this: "If you want to know the rest of this secret, call me." (Leave your number.)
- When you're at a restaurant, send someone you like a small appetizer with a funny note.
- Ask someone for help; for example, request directions to a nice dance place or restaurant in your area.
- Offer to help someone: Open a door, lend a pen, or give advice and recommendations.
- Walk a dog or play with a child at the park and meet people who like animals and children.
- Bring a book to a café or party and start reading. Others may ask what you're reading.
- Wear a T-shirt that's printed with a slogan for a cause you believe in: SAVE THE WHALES!
- Demonstrate your talents and abilities—play the piano, sing, perform magic tricks, analyze people's handwriting.
- Carry a camera with you, and ask the person you're interested in to take your picture. Offer to take your new friend's picture and mail him or her the photo.
- Ask a simple question like How's it going?

Whatever you decide to do, make sure it's within your comfort zone and fits your personality. If it's not you, it's not going to work.

Dating Services, Personal Ads, and the Internet

Because shy people are often self-conscious and anxious about meeting others in the normal course of their days, they often resort to private, less threatening alternatives, like dating services, personal ads, and the Internet. Although these alternatives can make things easier, they're not panaceas for all your dating problems. Regardless of which method you choose, you still have to meet that person face-to-face at some point. You'll still have to demonstrate good communication skills and act spontaneously from your Actor. And, ultimately, you'll still have to be compatible with that person. More-over, in today's society, with all the legitimate concerns about sexually transmitted diseases, personal safety, and the integrity of dating partners, it's a good idea to screen people carefully until it's clear they're safe, sincere, and worthy of your interest.

Rather than take your chances dating people you know little about—individuals whose primary qualification is that they answered your ad or paid money to join a dating service—spend time getting to know people in more meaningful ways by participating in ongoing events, activities, classes, and groups.

Although it's usually better to meet people through these larger group structures, there is one good thing about dating services, personal ads, and the like: They can help out-of-practice shy and Introverted people come out of their shells and get back into the dating scene.

Among the popular dating alternatives, the Internet—with its free and low-cost dating sites, twenty-four-hour chat areas, and E-mail options—appears to offer the most intriguing dating possibilities for shy people. The Internet can be a great confidence booster for shy people because they're not hampered by their appearance and self-consciousness when they're on-line. They can be flirty, fun-loving, and exactly the type of dating diva or ladies' man they would love to be in real life.

Nobody knows that the shy person hasn't had a real date in a year, a real relationship in five. The only thing that matters is the shy person's ability to chat on-line—to string words together by typing them on a computer screen. Since shy people are usually intelligent, reflective, and sensitive—and many are good writers—Internet chatting is often a piece of cake for them. In fact, the Internet may be the one place in their lives where they can allow their true romantic personalities to shine. There is no need to be self-conscious because there is no one staring back, just a blank computer screen they can use to create any image or persona they desire.

Although the Internet offers certain dating advantages, it's still not a cure-all. First of all, no matter how witty and confident shy people are on-line, they still need to meet and communicate with a potential partner in person if they want a real relationship. When they're face-to-face with that individual, and their Observer makes an unwanted appearance, shy people need to know how to switch into their Actor to save the day.

Moreover, shy people need to realize that not everyone they meet on-line is going to be honest with them. Because the anonymity of the Internet makes it easy to shade the truth, there will always be people who try to make themselves seem better by lying about their age, looks, career, finances, marital status, and so forth.

If you decide to go out with someone from the Internet, make sure you meet at a safe and neutral place the first few times. Go for coffee or conversation at a nearby diner or bookstore, and take your time getting to know this person. Also, make sure you are honest about yourself; resist the temptation to exaggerate to impress a potential mate. It's much better to tell the truth about yourself from the very beginning because, when you're honest up front, there won't be any surprises, and you will have laid the foundation for a trusting intimate relationship.

Telephone Dating Tactics for the Shy Person

Few things cause more frustration and confusion for shy people than knowing how to use the telephone in dating situations. Some shy men, for instance, have an obsession with getting a phone number from an attractive lady and then never ask for it. Others are able to get a phone number but never call. And then there are those who do call but leave such disjointed, rambling messages that even the CIA can't figure them out.

Shy women also have a problem with the whole phone issue. Many shy women, for instance, are reluctant to give out their phone numbers even if they really like the guy, because they don't feel they know him well enough. Others will give their phone numbers, then obsess: Will he call? When will he call? Finally, if he should happen to call and leave a message, they wonder how quickly they should return his call. They think: If I call too soon, he'll think I'm easy and desperate. If I wait too long, he'll think I'm not interested and he'll move on.

To avoid the phone trap, try something different: When you meet someone you're interested in, make a casual and indirect invitation, and see how your new acquaintance responds. You can, for example, mention a place where you like to hang out and ask him or her to join you. You can say something like this: "I'm usually at Borders at seven o'clock on Thursdays for the book signings and talks. If you want to drop by, you can say hi and check out a great talk." Have one of the Borders business cards handy, and give it to the person so he or she has the address and phone number of the meeting place. This is a low-pressure way to spend more time with someone you just met and works well because there are no expectations. If he shows up, fine. If he doesn't, that's OK; you were going to be there anyway.

If you happen to be more Introverted and don't get out that much, you may instead want to give the person your personal or business card so he or she can call you. Before you do this, however, make sure this individual seems genuinely interested in meeting you again. You can, for example, ask your new acquaintance if he or she would like to get together for a mutual interest (maybe both of you like jazz and there's a concert next weekend). If the person appears interested, offer your card so he or she can call you to confirm the appointment.

Many shy people, especially shy men, give away their cards too eagerly, then are surprised when they aren't called. Keep this in mind: No one is going to be more interested in you just because you gave her or him a card. Give out your VIP card only to someone who seems genuinely interested in spending more time with you.

Now let's assume your new acquaintance calls you and leaves a message, and you call him or her back. But, instead of talking with your prospective honey, you get the dreaded answering machine. Do you leave a message? If so, what do you say? Ideally, you'll call at different times during the day or evening until your new acquaintance picks up the phone and you speak to him or her directly.

I know what you're thinking: What if I don't want to speak to that gorgeous stranger in person? What if it's easier—and much less intimidating—to leave a message? Of course it's easier, but leaving messages all the time doesn't help you grow as a shy person. It's much better to talk in person.

First of all, telephone conversations are a good way for you to practice your Actor. When you're on the phone, you don't have to see that irresistible man or woman in person, and you won't be so intimidated by his or her good looks and direct eye contact. Moreover, when you talk on the phone, you can feel your new acquaintance out and determine if he or she is really interested in you. That way you don't have to waste time leaving messages for someone who isn't really interested.

However, if for some reason you can't get through after a few attempts (or if you're just too shy to talk to the individual), go ahead and leave a message. Try not to make it overly sentimental or clinging. Avoid saying things like "I loved meeting you; I can't wait till we meet again." Either leave a quick name and phone number message or try a funny, cute one if it suits your personality. If, for example, you know the person likes John Gray's book *Men Are from Mars, Women Are from Venus*, you can say, "This is Mars calling Venus. How are *you* feeling today?"

Another important issue is timing. When should you call? When should you return a call? Some dating manuals advise you to call no sooner than three days after meeting a new person. They also tell you to wait at least three days before you return his or her call. According to these "dating experts," calling sooner would make you seem desperate and needy.

Nonsense. There's no law that establishes the best time to call a potential romantic partner; it's entirely up to you. In fact, your best approach is to call when you feel like it. The advice here is not to tailor your personality to meet somebody else's expectations but to be yourself from the very start and do what feels right for you. If you do what comes naturally, you will discover, up front, if this person is really right for you. You will know, right now, if the two of you are compatible and have the strong chemistry that's needed to make the relationship work in the long run.

Shy Dates:
Where to Go, What to Do

When it comes to dates, especially first dates, try low-pressure, inexpensive outings like taking a walk. The beauty of a walk is that it's perfectly suited for a shy person's temperament. First of all, you're doing something active, so you're in your Actor mode, and your Observer won't butt in as much to make you feel self-conscious. Another advantage is that you can ease into the walk. You don't have to make a big announcement. You can just start walking from whatever location you met your date and then continue walking and talking as you take in the scenery.

Walking makes for an excellent first date because it gives you the chance to get to know your new friend in a slow, relaxed way. Plus walking is very versatile: While you're carrying on a nice conversation, you and your partner can walk in a zoo, street fair, or carnival. You can stroll around a lake or down a trail. Or you can walk and window-shop; if you get hungry, you can stop for food at a bakery or sandwich shop and munch away to your heart's content.

Here's another fun idea: Build the anticipation by sending your date something to remind him or her of where you're going and all the fun you'll be having. If, for example, you have a concert date planned, leave a cassette of the band's music at your friend's workplace during the week. If you're going to an art gallery, send your friend a postcard with some of the paintings you will see there.

For a more relaxed and conventional evening, you can rent videos, or listen to lectures or concerts at your local community college.

Rejection:
The Nine-Letter Word

We've come to the last, and perhaps most important, consideration for shy people who are dating: rejection. Because shy people are often afraid of being rejected in social situations, they may not try to meet new people, and they may retreat from those who are interested in meeting them.

The reason shy people fear rejection so much is they don't understand the true nature of dating. When people turn you down for a date, or when they don't appear to be all that interested in you, they're not rejecting you personally. What they're really saying is that, at that precise moment, they don't believe you have what they need, whether it's a certain look, a particular way of talking, or whatever.

Their reaction has nothing to do with your ultimate value as a human being or your worthiness as a romantic partner. They are simply telling you there is a fundamental mismatch between what you have to offer and what they want at that moment. Although your shy-sensitive nature is a valuable personal resource, it may not be seen as such by certain people. If that's the case, so be it. The good news is that there are a select few individuals out there who will not only appreciate what you have to offer but will revere and cherish you for it. It is from this small, elite pool of people that you will choose your soul mate.

When it doesn't work out with someone, don't consider it a rejection. Regard it as a nonevent, a nonhappening. You and the other person didn't mesh because the necessary ingredients weren't present. You don't need to be angry, hurt, or disappointed. It's just a nonoccurrence, the absence of a chemical reaction, that's all. Do you think a doctor feels rejected because her patient happens to be healthy? Do you think an insurance agent suffers a loss of prestige because his client is already adequately covered? Of course not. They don't have any pretensions that they can satisfy everyone's needs, and neither should you.

You don't have to satisfy the needs of every man or woman on the planet; you don't need to be desired by all. You only have to satisfy the needs of one person: the love of your life, that ideal mate who will love you no matter what. If you can satisfy that one person, you will be happy, and all the so-called rejections in the world won't make one bit of difference. You've opened the one door you need to open; you've entered the one heart you need to enter.

Good luck, and happy shy dating.

CHAPTER 12

Dating Wisdom for the Stay-at-Home Introvert

To her friends thirty-two-year-old Michelle was quite a paradox: She was so much fun and so lively when they got together at each other's homes for barbecues, videos, and card games. She joked, talked, and laughed as if there was no tomorrow. But when it came to going out, Michelle suddenly became a party pooper. Most of the time she declined their invitations, saying she was too tired or busy. If they did manage to drag her out, Michelle was all right for a while, but then she would come up with an excuse to go home early.

The *real* reason Michelle avoided the social scene was that she hated going out to loud, smoky places to be around a crowd of strangers she had little in common with. She would much rather relax in her cozy home—soaking in the tub, listening to her favorite classical music, and playing on the Internet. Sure, having a few close friends over for a night of wine drinking and girl talk was also nice, but that was as far as she wanted to take her social life most of the time.

Feeling comfortable? Sure. Feeling a good man by her side? Big problem. Michelle knew her lifestyle wasn't exactly conducive to meeting desirable, eligible men. She just didn't get out enough, and her limited social circle wasn't helping matters much.

Although she was generally happy with her life, Michelle had to admit she felt lonely at times. It had been three long years since her last serious relationship, and she wondered how she could meet a good man without having to compromise her lifestyle. She wished she could find the answer because then her life would be so close to perfect.

Imagine a cozy little world made up of private thoughts, soft whispers, and plenty of time to reflect on daily occurrences and ponder life's deepest mysteries. In this safe little haven there would be no excessive chatter or loud distractions. There would be only simple quietness and room for one, maybe two, possibly three, of your closest friends, all of them like you, enjoying the things that come from within: meditating, listening, reading, watching, and, above all, thinking. This place you're envisioning is the private world of Introverts; those special individuals who get most of their energy from their own thoughts and who thrive on quiet and inward moments.

If you scored as an Introvert on the Shy Type Quiz in Chapter 4, you're the type of person who has a limited amount of social energy and who, instead of spending time with a lot of people in social activities, prefers to be by yourself at home or with a few close friends doing quiet, intimate, and mentally stimulating things.

Being an Introvert can give you definite romantic advantages. You're likely to be loyal, reflective, soft-spoken, trustworthy, deep, intelligent, well-read, and creative—all noteworthy attributes that will make you very desirable in the eyes of the right people.

As an Introvert, you are the type of person who looks within for sustenance. You don't need a lot of people in your life to be happy. Although you may have a few close friends, you can be perfectly satisfied with your own company. You may be quiet and inward, but there are times when you can be quite sociable and outgoing. You can even be the life of the party if you want to be. But everything depends on your supply of social energy.

When they have the desire and interest, Introverts (especially those who are not shy) can choose to spend their store of energy meeting people, networking, talking, laughing, telling jokes, and even running the show. But at some point they get tired; their energy runs out. When their social batteries are depleted, they don't feel like talking anymore. They long for the sweet comfort of home, their private little thought world, nurturing and reenergizing them until they feel whole and complete once more.

In the early twentieth century Carl Jung likened Introverts to turtles because both had thick shells that protected them from the external world. The shell of an Introvert, however, is not a physical one but a mental one. This protective shell is represented by the intense desire to go inside—into one's thoughts and inner life—whenever things get too hectic in the outside world.

Not all Introverts are the same, however. Some like to stay in most of the time; others can go either way, sometimes going out, sometimes staying home. Moreover, just because people are Introverts doesn't mean they never go out. Even strong Introverts like to come out of their shells once in a while to have some fun, meet people, and learn something new. Yet, despite their occasional outings, most strong Introverts do usually prefer to stay home a majority of the time.

Introverts also come in two varieties: shy and non-shy. On the one hand, there are the shy Introverts: those people who are quite sensitive and afraid of being judged and criticized in social situations. If their anxiety and embarrassment get too intense, they will retreat from the scene rapidly, doing everything possible to avoid rejection, criticism, and humiliation. On the other hand, there are the non-shy Introverts, those relatively thick-skinned people who aren't as easily hurt in social situations. Rather than retreat from social encounters to avoid being judged, non-shy Introverts tend to be comfortable, staying as long as their energy holds out.

Regardless of whether you're a shy or a non-shy Introvert, the truth remains the same: It's not easy to meet people and have an active romantic life when you're an Introvert. You may be bright, attractive, personable, and kind. You may be well-educated and come from a good family. You may have a good job and loyal, trustworthy friends. But when you're an Introvert there's always something missing, something that prevents you from having the successful romantic life you deserve. That "something" is actually two things: social energy and social structure.

Social energy is the amount of psychological energy you have for social situations, the vitality and force of mind you bring to social encounters. As an Introvert you have a limited amount of social energy. Every phone call, every visitor, every social activity uses up more of this energy until you feel drained and depleted. When your store of social energy is completely used up, you will feel tired and listless, and you will need to retreat into your inner world to recharge and revitalize yourself.

Social energy is such a crucial component of your social life because it can affect so many things: how many social activities you attend, how many friends you have, how many new people you meet, and whether you will have the opportunity to meet and develop a lasting relationship with a compatible partner.

Despite its importance, many Introverts don't know how to use their social energy properly. Some Introverts hoard all their social energy and rarely if ever go out. Although they feel more comfortable and energized at home, they end up handicapping themselves by limiting their social exposure and greatly reducing their odds of meeting a romantic partner. Introverts also waste valuable social energy on situations and people that aren't likely to bring them the results they want. They may, for example, talk enthusiastically to a married couple for two hours while neglecting the attractive single person who is sitting all alone.

The other thing many Introverts lack is social structure: being part of a social group or network that makes it easy for them to meet available romantic partners. Because Introverts get so much of their energy from within, they don't typically need or want to get involved in group situations where they have to deal with a lot of people. In fact, being around too many people for too long can be tiring and overwhelming for Introverts. This doesn't mean Introverts dislike people; they enjoy human interaction as much as anyone else. The difference is that they prefer to choose their friends carefully and spend their precious time and energy with a few special people in comfortable and private settings. Another reason Introverts avoid groups is that they're usually quite independent. Rather than wait for a friend to call, Introverts can be perfectly content going to a movie or dinner by themselves. Finally, Introverts are often resistant to getting enmeshed in group social structures because they place such a high value on their private, quiet time.

But there is a price to pay for such comfort and privacy: Introverts don't usually get invited to the best parties, they don't get introductions to interesting people, and they don't usually meet romantic partners through their friends, who are often Introverts just like them.

Energy:
The Fuel for Social Excellence

Carol, a non-shy, Introverted thirty-five-year-old tax accountant, was a giving person in many ways. She gave generously to charities, lent money to her friends, and always had a few dollars for the homeless people who panhandled downtown, where she worked. There was one area in her life, however, where Carol was quite stingy. When it came to spending her social energy, Carol was like a miser who hoarded every penny.

As a strong Introvert, she had a limited amount of social energy, and she was very careful about how she spent it. She especially disliked making small talk or spending nights in loud, crowded places crammed with strangers; to Carol, these situations were energy drainers that offered little in return. She much preferred quiet nights in, spent with a few close friends or by herself—reading, writing, thinking, and doing yoga.

Although she was generally happy with her lifestyle, there was something missing: It had been five years since her last relationship, and Carol realized she needed to make some adjustments in her social life. Following the advice of a friend ("Introducing friends to each other is an excellent way to get socially connected and meet someone yourself"), Carol decided to introduce some of her friends and acquaintances to each other to see what would happen. Not only did they enjoy themselves (one couple even got engaged), but Carol found that in the next several weeks one of her grateful friends introduced her to two fine men.

Although extending her social energy like this took some effort, Carol had to admit she was enjoying the results. She's still casually dating both of the guys she was introduced to, and she knows she is bound to meet Mr. Right as long as she continues to project her energy into the social world.

The word *energy* is used a lot in everyday conversation. Some people say they lack energy; others say they overflow with it. Some people bring you good energy; others bring you bad.

As an Introvert, you have two kinds of energy: social energy and thought energy. Social energy is the energy you need for social encounters, the psychological fuel you use to remain talkative, animated, and involved in social encounters. As an Introvert, your social energy is usually exhausted pretty rapidly. Once it's gone you need to go somewhere by yourself and recharge. As an Introvert, you recharge by going within and getting energy from your own thoughts, your thought energy.

Think about it: Have you ever been in a fun social environment but then, right in the middle of having a good time, you felt tired and emotionally drained without knowing why? No matter how much fun you were having, you knew you didn't have enough energy to keep it going. What did you do? Maybe you went home and read. Or you took a long walk in the still night. Or you got in your car, turned on the radio, and went for a drive. And then everything changed. All of a sudden you felt energized again; vital, alive, ready to do more, eager to take on the world. With your thought energy revitalizing you, you now had more social energy to go around. If you wanted to, you could have gone back to that social event and picked up right where you left off.

That's the way it works for Introverts: Their thought energy gives them more social energy. This is an important point to keep in mind when you're out. If you find that your social energy is starting to drag, give yourself a thought energy break: Go for a short walk or sit in a quiet corner for a while. This way, you'll remain active, alert, and energized for longer periods. Instead of leaving the social event early and missing out on a great opportunity to meet a fine person, you will be able to stay longer because you have more thought energy backing you up.

Another challenge you face as an Introvert is getting out in the first place. When you're in your relaxed, safe haven—listening to your favorite CDs, reading your favorite books—your social energy just seems to contract naturally. Instead of disturbing your calm balance by going out, you would much rather stay in and follow the direction in which your energy is leading you—inside yourself. But sometimes you just have to push yourself to get out of the house, to go out and talk to people. Sometimes you just have to Extravert yourself if you want to make improvements in your social life.

Exercise 1. Expanding Your Social Energy: Pushing the House

In this exercise you will learn how to switch your social energy on when you need it, even though your inward-pulling thought energy is urging you to stay home.

STEP 1. Find a comfortable place, sit down, and close your eyes. Imagine that all your energy is encompassed in a clear plastic bubble and that you're sitting comfortably inside this bubble. This bubble is your mental house, your psychological abode. This is where you live; where you get your life sustenance; where you park all your feelings, desires, goals, and dreams.

Imagine that, just outside this clear bubble, you see the most desirable person you could ever hope for. He or she is kind, gorgeous, generous, loving, and just your type.

Further imagine that, in your desire to meet this person, you begin to push the plastic bubble outward—expanding it, extending it, making it bigger and bigger—until the fantastic person is sitting inside the bubble next to you, holding your hand and gazing into your eyes. As you imagine this, be fully aware of any feelings you're experiencing, whether it's euphoria, joy, love, pleasure, ecstasy, or the like.

STEP 2. Whenever you're tempted to stay home instead of going out and meeting new people, repeat Step 1. Imagine that, by pushing your energy bubble outward, you're giving yourself the opportunity to connect with an awesome person, the man or woman of your dreams. This will be exactly the motivation you need to step out of your comfort zone.

STEP 3. To create even more social energy in your life, try the powerful technique known as Energetic Dating. It works like this: Think of several people you know and decide which ones would be best for each other in a romantic relationship. Offer to introduce your most compatible friends and acquaintances to each other.

Whether your friends decide to go out with each other doesn't matter. What matters is that, by offering to set them up on dates, you have converted some of your thought energy into social energy. When you do this, you will open up some interesting possibilities.

Now some of your friends will want to give the same social energy back to you by introducing you to some of their friends and acquaintances. Even if they don't, the mere act of introducing people to each other will create a positive flow of social energy into your life. This energy will eventually manifest itself in the form of invitations, introductions, and new friendships. When you extend your social energy out to others like this, a lot of good things will happen to you; just wait.

Social Structure:
The Foundation of a Rewarding
Romantic Life

"How do I break out of my shell?" asked Florence, an attractive Introvert who came to me for dating advice. "I really enjoy staying home with my books and computer. But I don't meet anyone at home, except the postman, and he's already taken."

Most people would be surprised to learn that Florence was still single at thirty-one. A beautiful, statuesque brunette with flowing dark hair, a pleasing voice, and a honey bear personality, she was also fluent in four languages, had an IQ of 160, and was a business whiz.

Yet when it came to her social life, her Introverted nature kept her date book running on empty. Sure, more than a few strangers hit on her at grocery stores and post offices, but she didn't want any part of that.

"You need to immerse yourself in the right type of social structure," I told her. "Join a respected humanitarian group you would be proud to be a part of. There you'll make friends with men who have high morals, and you'll get to know them over time."

Florence eventually joined a church group whose mission was to bring food and toys to poor children in Mexico on a monthly basis. She loved being part of the group and greatly respected the work they were doing. Every smile from the children made her feel grateful to be involved in such a worthy cause. It also made her heart happy to be in the company of such strong, caring men who were dedicated to helping those who were less fortunate.

After six months of volunteering, Florence became good friends with several single men from the group. She knows it's only a matter of time before God chooses the right man for her and joins them in holy matrimony. In the meantime she is happy to focus on her noble mission: to help the hurting children of Mexico and make a lasting impact on their lives.

If energy is the key that unlocks the door of romantic possibilities, structure is the home that waits inside, the foundation of your romantic success.

Throughout history human beings have banded together in various structures—tribes, families, and villages—for many reasons, ranging from physical survival and economic necessity to emotional connection and a sense of belonging. Today, with the emphasis on technology, privacy, and individuality, many people are living increasingly isolated lives, without any significant sense of group structure or support. Gradually, the old social networks are being replaced by cyber-communities: groups of people who share similar interests and communicate with each other on the Internet but who usually have little, if any, sustained personal contact.

This trend toward a more private, Introverted, technology-based society does have benefits: People can live more freely, independently, and creatively because they no longer have to depend so much on social groups for approval and support. They can receive satisfaction from within and create the lifestyle they prefer without having to conform to group expectations.

At the same time, when you do everything by yourself things can get pretty tough, especially in your dating life. If you have to do all the dating work on your own—talking to people, setting up options like dating services, and so forth—you will often feel overwhelmed and frustrated. You will start to wonder: Isn't there an easier way to connect with people?

Yes, there is. If you want to have an active and fulfilling romantic life, your best bet is to join a well-established social structure: a group of like-minded individuals who come together regularly for a common purpose. When you play a significant role in a social structure like a church group, community organization, or nonprofit charity, you will enjoy many built-in benefits.

First of all, when you're part of any well-developed social structure you will have the opportunity to meet a large number of people. Because others recognize you as one of them, they will be open to getting better acquainted. Once you're an accepted part of the group, it's an easy matter for you to use your shy type detective skills (see Chapter 10) to pinpoint and meet the best romantic candidates for you.

Another great advantage is that the other group members can introduce you to potential partners. If you know one of the members well enough, you can mention that you're single and looking, and before long this person may introduce you to someone you really like. In fact, being introduced by a trusted friend is one of the best ways to meet someone. Not only do you come with a word of approval—thereby lessening your new friend's anxiety about meeting you—but the person you're meeting comes with a recommendation too.

Finally, when you're a member of a group, you can get to know people over time and see how they react in various situations. When you see someone regularly, and perhaps work with that person on a project or activity, you see that person as he or she really is. You can then answer some of these crucial questions:

- Does this person have a temper?
- How does he or she react under pressure?
- Is this person gentle, sensitive, and giving?
- Is this person loyal?
- Is he or she generous?
- Is this individual honest?
- Does he or she have integrity?

Why Introverts Pay a Price
When They Fly Solo

Whereas you will usually feel more secure and comfortable (and know a lot more about a person) when you meet through a respectable group structure, things are much different when you meet a new person on your own. You're in a far weaker position when you meet somebody using the Introvert's typical one-stop dating methods: meeting people blindly through paid dating options (personal ads, dating services, and the like) or by chance at the grocery or Laundromat, at nightclubs or parties.

First, there's the pressure. When you meet someone in a random situation (let's say while having coffee at Starbucks), the chances are good that you will never see this person again. This is doubly true if you're an Introvert who rarely gets out and is not likely to be back at the same place any time soon. Because you know this is probably the last time you will ever see this person, you feel pressured to make a good impression. Now, as you gaze at Mr. Gorgeous, your Observer will start pestering you: "Oh my God. What should I say? What should I do? He's probably going to leave in a couple of minutes, and I'll never see him again. Should I ask for his phone number? No, too bold. Should I give him mine? Yes, but I need to wait until he asks. Oh, no, he's getting ready to leave."

The torture continues until the person does leave, and you're sitting alone with dashed expectations and a lukewarm cup of coffee.

But that's not the worst part. What if you do give him your phone number and go out with him? What do you really know about him? Sure, he can be charming for a few minutes at Starbucks, but what if he's a tyrant, irresponsible, and hard to get along with? What if he turns out to be your worst nightmare?

It's easy to see why dating people without the benefit of a social structure can be inefficient, risky, and time-consuming. (How many Starbucks coffees do you have to drink before you run across someone you can connect with?) Yet many Introverts still insist on going solo. For the most part Introverts resist the idea of joining a group structure because they don't want to give up their private time and independent lifestyle.

Think about your own experiences: When was the last time you were a regular member of an ongoing group where you spent time with people based on a common interest, cause, or goal? Maybe you were on the journalism or yearbook staff in high school. Perhaps you joined a fraternity or sorority in college. Or you may have been part of a Rotary club, Toastmasters, or Chamber of Commerce when you started working. If you're like most people, you probably had some good opportunities to be part of a group social structure when you were in school, but most of those opportunities dried up after you graduated and joined the workforce. Although you may have participated in your share of group activities when you were younger, now that you're a grown-up Introvert, you may have a natural aversion to group activities because you prefer doing things on your own.

For those of you who think this way, consider this: Without a strong group structure backing you up, you will be hard-pressed to achieve your romantic goals and meet the person of your dreams. This doesn't mean you can't date people and find lovers and romantic partners on your own; you probably can. But the advantages are so great when you participate in a group structure that you would find it very difficult, if not impossible, to duplicate the same results on your own.

Because Introverts have limited social circles and usually go out with a small number of people during their romantic careers, they don't have much of a mental measuring stick to compare their current romantic partner with. They may think a partner is just fine when, in reality, he or she is far from great. At the same time, many Introverts realize they have a limited amount of energy for dating, and they know that they may not have that many dating opportunities left. Even if they're attractive, intelligent, and personable, Introverts are well aware of the equation that states: Limited social exposure = few dates = few romantic opportunities = loneliness.

Yet regardless of how limited your dating opportunities have been in the past, the worst thing you can do is settle for someone who is not your ideal just because you don't think you can do any better, or because you don't want to exert any more effort or wait any longer. Too many Introverts end up marrying incompatible partners because they were too eager to get the whole dating and marriage thing over with. They fell in love with the first individual who offered them some attention and affection, only to discover later that this person was totally wrong for them. Instead of committing yourself to the first interesting person who crosses your path, you're much better off dating a substantial number of people until you can find that one who is truly compatible with you.

Exercise 2. Building the Ideal Social Structure

Here's an exercise to help you create the best social structure so you can meet the person you're looking for.

STEP 1. For the next four weeks keep a written log of all the Introvert and Extravert time you spend each day after coming home from work or school. Introvert time consists of private, inward activities you do on your own, like reading, writing, and working around the house. Extravert time is the time you spend in the outside world or socializing with people: going to parties, having lunch with a friend, taking a class.

Make columns for the date, time spent, activity, and Introvert/Extravert category. Your log may look something like this:

Date	Hours	Activity	Introvert (I)/Extravert (E)
6/3	2	Reading	I
	3	Watching TV	I
	1	Dinner with friend	E

In this example, on June 3 you spent five hours of Introvert time and one hour of Extravert time after work.

At the end of the week, add up your Introvert and Extravert hours and convert them to percentages. Write down the total hours and percentages of Introvert/Extravert time at the bottom of the page. For example, during the week that ended on June 10, let's say you had a total of fifty hours of leisure time. You spent forty of those hours on Introvert activities (writing, reading, meditating, eating alone, and relaxing) and ten hours on Extravert activities (going to a dinner party, window-shopping at the mall with a friend), for a combination of 80 percent Introvert and 20 percent Extravert time.

Don't be concerned if you aren't spending a lot of time on Extraverted activities each week. The amount of time you spend is not as important as the types of Extraverted activities you spend time on. For example, spending only 10 to 20 percent of your time on Extraverted activities is perfectly fine, as long as they're the right ones—situations in which you feel comfortable and that enable you to meet available, compatible singles.

STEP 2. Think of all the groups you have joined in the past, especially those that provided you with a strong sense of accomplishment and belonging. Also, think of some groups that you never joined but that interested you because of their activities. Write these down.

STEP 3. Consider some groups you can join right now that are the same as or similar to the ones you listed in Step 2. If, for example, you enjoyed being part of student government in high school, perhaps you can help out on a political campaign. If you had fun writing for the college newspaper, maybe you can volunteer to work for your community newspaper.

Choose the top three groups based on how much you think you would enjoy yourself if you were a member. When considering which group you would enjoy the most, evaluate the likelihood of meeting compatible singles there. Some groups have a higher percentage of married people, others have more singles. You will undoubtedly enjoy yourself a lot more in the group that does the kind of things you enjoy and also has a significant number of singles.

Write down your top three groups on a sheet of paper, and circle your number one choice; this is the one you will investigate first.

STEP 4. Look at your Introvert/Extravert log from Step 1. Based on the average number of Extravert hours you spent in the last four weeks, decide how much time you will use for your new group activity. If, for example, you normally spend ten Extravert hours per week (and that number feels comfortable), you may decide to commit three hours per week to your top choice, the newspaper, while using the rest of your hours on your usual Extravert activities, like going out to dinner with friends.

Now write the number of hours you will spend on the group you've selected in your log.

STEP 5. Get involved in the group you have chosen, and spend the Extravert time you have decided to spend. You may need to adjust your hours somewhat, and you may want to experiment with different groups until you find the right one. In time you will find a social structure in which you can grow and comfortably and efficiently be with the types of people who meet your standards.

From Me to We:
Moving Toward a Rewarding
Love Relationship

In the last few chapters we've gone deeply into you—your concerns, needs, and goals as a shy or Introverted person. Now it's time to complete the picture and see what it's like when you add a second person, a partner who will bring joy and happiness into your life. This is your final step, and perhaps your most challenging one: to connect deeply with another human being in a long-term relationship.

For many shy and Introverted people, forming a deep love bond with another human being represents a life-altering transition— from solo to duo, from me to we, from one person who thinks only about his or her needs to two people who participate in a mature, loving, give-and-take relationship. If you've been alone most of your life—or if you're now alone after a breakup or divorce—you know it's not an easy thing to give up your independence to be with another person. Although you may often have dreamed of being united with a special partner for life, chances are you've also been afraid of it at the same time.

In the back of your mind you may have had questions like these:

- Will I have to give up my true nature to be loved by this person?
- Will he or she hurt me?
- Can I trust this person?
- Will this person love me forever?

We're about to explore your concerns about being in a long-term relationship. We will also examine what it takes to create and maintain a successful relationship that fulfills your heart's desires.

Yes, it's scary. Sure, it's challenging. But it's also satisfying, healing, and life-changing. Get ready; it's time to settle in with the love of your life.

CHAPTER 13

Creating the Successful Shy-Romantic Relationship

The bathtub was filled with deliciously warm water, playful bubbles, fragrant rose petals, and of course, Hector and Evonne, two shy people in love. As they took turns scrubbing each other's backs, not a word was said, not a sound was needed. Every facial expression was a word, every gesture a complete sentence. Shyly, tenderly, they caressed each other and made slow, passionate love in the tub. After drying each other off, they cuddled in bed and relaxed in each other's arms.

Tonight was their one-year wedding anniversary, and they couldn't have been happier. From the moment they met at a shyness clinic two and a half years ago, they realized they were meant for each other. Although they were sure from the very beginning, there were doubters who weren't so sure and told them so. "You'll get bored with each other; you're too much alike. Someone has to be the boss, someone has to be the follower," declared the naysayers.

It was true that Hector and Evonne were very much alike. Both were quiet, shy, sensitive types who enjoyed relaxed evenings by the fireplace, reading together, watching videos, and talking. Gentle and loving, these kind souls also detested conflict, and hated the fights and arguments they'd gotten into with their previous partners. They both wanted the same thing: a respectful, loving, conflict-free relationship.

Ironically, many of the "friends" who had warned them against their relationship were now divorced and asking them for relationship advice. But none of that mattered now. The only thing that made any sense was their cozy little world—their sweet cocoon of intertwined bodies, hearts, and souls—as they vowed to cherish and love each other for the rest of their lives.

To be in love, to build a marriage and family that brings joy, happiness, and a sense of meaning and purpose to one's life—this is the dream of many shy and Introverted people. There is nothing purer, more beautiful, and more transcendent. Yet for many shy people the idea of having such a relationship is as downright scary as it is exciting. The scary part for many shy people is the thought of letting a person deep into their hearts. By opening up their souls to another person, shy people often feel exposed and vulnerable, fearful that this new person in their lives will violate their trust and hurt them deeply.

To break through these barriers to intimacy, shy people need to learn to trust themselves as well as their partners. They need to trust themselves first by embracing their shy nature and selecting a compatible mate (see Chapter 10 for tips) who truly respects and appreciates their gift of shyness. Shy people also need to learn how to trust their partners—to open their hearts fully—so they can develop a deep, long-lasting love. Trust is all-important for shy people because they have such a strong need for security. They need to feel safe and secure in the arms of the one person who will shield them from the harshness of the world.

Then there's the matter of sex. Few things cause more anxiety in shy people than the prospect of having sex with their partner, especially at the beginning of a relationship. Recognizing, and dealing with, these fears and insecurities is vital if you want to develop a satisfying, long-term relationship.

Although you may not be in a relationship at the moment, it's a good idea to read this chapter now so you will know what to expect when you do find that ideal person.

Trust: The Seeds of Intimacy

Intimacy is a thing of beauty. To share your deepest feelings with another human being—to trust and love someone implicitly with all your heart—is one of the most thrilling, deeply satisfying, and soul-expanding experiences you'll ever have. But it can also be frightening. Especially if you're a shy person who has been alone for most of your life, who has gone to great lengths to keep people from getting inside your sensitive core because you were terrified they would hurt you, then discard you like a day-old newspaper.

For shy people, being intimate with a romantic partner is like giving that person the key to a safe-deposit box that contains their most valuable treasures. If the person they trust happens to be a crook, their entire life's fortune will be stolen, and they won't be able to do anything about it. When it's gone, it's gone forever. That's why so many shy people put up those wall-to-wall psychological barriers, those thick shells that keep other people from getting in. That's why shy people end conversations too soon, fail to return phone calls (or fail to make them in the first place), and generally avoid available and attractive people. They're so terrified of being hurt and rejected that they will do everything in their power to keep people from getting too close.

One of the ways shy people push others away is by setting impossibly high standards when it comes to choosing their prospective mates. Some shy people insist that their mate must look like Adonis or Ms. Universe, have a Harvard Ph.D., be a millionaire, and have absolutely no bad habits. In a word, perfect. The truth is that shy people aren't usually picky just to be picky. Rather, their stringent selection process is another way to protect themselves from being hurt. They're afraid to let a real person get too close because that would make them vulnerable and give the other person the power to hurt them.

Yet one thing could turn everything around for shy people and move them toward a satisfying intimate relationship. That thing is trust: the wholehearted belief, and confidence, in someone or something. There's no getting around it: If you want to experience love, you must first experience trust. To develop this trust, you need to examine closely three things: the facts about your partner, your own intuition about him or her, and your ability to trust in a mate.

Exercise 1. Trusting the Facts

Trust shouldn't be blind; it should be based, in large part, on the facts—on what you see, hear, and learn about this person who may become your lifelong mate. As you learn more about your potential partner, your goal is to obtain enough evidence to determine whether this person is truly compatible with you, as well as honest, reliable, physically and emotionally healthy, and willing to commit to you.

Here are a few steps you can take to gather the information you need.

STEP 1. Give your prospective mate the Shy Type Quiz, LoveType Quiz (from my book *LoveTypes*), or any other personality questionnaire you think will provide you with valuable information about his or her personality and temperament. Your task is to determine whether you're likely to be compatible with this person in a long-term relationship.

One caveat: Don't turn the testing into an overly serious "I'll dump you, if you don't pass" task. Make it fun; treat it like a game. You may want to try some of the free personality and relationship compatibility tests on the Internet. You can take these tests with your mate and receive immediate results.

When evaluating the test results, your goal is not necessarily to find someone who is identical to you, but someone who is compatible with you in the important areas of the relationship (read some good books on relationship compatibility, such as Barbara De Angelis's *Are You the One for Me?*). When someone is fundamentally compatible with you, you will find that your relationship is more harmonious because you have much less to fight about and a lot more in common.

STEP 2. See how the person behaves in the real world, especially under pressure. What happens when the tire goes flat? Does he get agitated and angry, or does he play it cool? How about when she's late for an appointment. Does she snap at you, or is she still her loving self?

SPECIAL TIP. Enlist your partner's help for a project or activity and see how well you work together. It doesn't have to be anything big or complicated, just something the two of you can do together (painting a small room, bringing food to poor people) that will give you additional insight into your partner's character.

STEP 3. Talk to people who know this person; ask their candid and confidential opinion about your potential partner. You may want to talk to your partner's family members, friends, acquaintances, co-workers, and so forth. This can be a little tricky because his or her friends and family will probably say only good things about the person. Moreover, they may tell your partner about your questions. But if you choose the right person—someone who's not a blabbermouth and who appears to be fair-minded—and do your interviewing in a subtle, indirect manner, you can pick up a lot of information not only from what is said but from what isn't. If, for example, you ask whether your partner is the jealous type, and his friend changes the subject abruptly, it may be a clue that your partner indeed has a jealous bone in his body.

As you do your investigation, take each discovery with a grain of salt. You don't want to make your relationship decision solely on the basis of the sniping of one disgruntled friend or the results of one quickie personality test on the Internet. But keep adding things up, double-checking the facts, and seeing where the evidence leads you. Your objective is to find out as much as you can about this person so you can determine whether he or she is really your best match.

Exercise 2. Trusting Yourself

Once you're satisfied that you've obtained enough background information about your prospective mate, you still need to look within yourself to answer the all-important question: Is this the right person for me?

Up to 90 percent of your decision may be based on what you've directly observed and learned about this person's habits, health, values, preferences, personality, character, interests, and finances. The all-important remaining 10 percent is the knowledge you may not immediately detect about someone, things that are buried deep within that person's nature and may not come out until much later. This is where your intuition comes in handy.

Although your intuition is usually on target, you may not always have trusted it because you let the Observer confuse you. You may have intuitively known that someone was right for you (or wrong for you), but you didn't follow your intuition because the Observer got in the way. The following exercise will help you trust your intuition more, especially when it comes to determining whether somebody is really the one for you.

STEP 1. Sit on a couch or chair, get comfortable, and relax. Think back to a time (or times) when you had a gut hunch about someone, an intuitive feeling, and you were right on the money. Maybe from the first moment you met someone you had a strong feeling that you couldn't trust this person, and before long you were proven right; your "friend" turned out to be a liar and cheat. On another occasion you met someone and had the opposite reaction: You immediately felt at ease; you knew you could trust this person. And later your feelings were confirmed when this person turned out to be a terrific individual and you became the best of friends.

Write these experiences down in a notebook, and include as much detail as possible.

STEP 2. Think back to the first time you met the person you're with. Recall the time, place, and mood you were in. Remember what both of you were wearing, how you met, what was said.

Now clear your mind of everything but this image, and ask yourself: How did I feel about this person when I first met him or her? Did I feel I could trust this person?

STEP 3. Recall the most recent time you were with your partner. Remember what was said as well as how you felt during the interaction.

Now answer the following questions: How do I feel about this person right now? Do I feel I can trust this person with my love and my life?

Take your time answering these questions, and take the answers seriously. Don't try to talk yourself out of what you've just learned from your intuition. If your answer is a clear "yes, I can trust this person," then proceed to Exercise 3 and continue to build up the trust you have for your partner. If your answer is unclear or a definite no, then you need to look at the information you gathered in Exercise 1 and continue meditating on whether you should continue this relationship.

Maybe you'll come to the conclusion—based on your fact gathering and intuition—that this person is not for you. If that's the case, you're better off starting over and finding someone who does have the qualities you're looking for.

Exercise 3. Trusting Your Mate

If you believe someone is right for you (he or she passed the tests in Exercises 1 and 2) but you still have a problem trusting this person because of your own fears, do this exercise.

STEP 1. Find a quiet room in your house and tell your mate that you will be doing an exercise in building trust. Now put on a blindfold and stand in front of your mate with your back to him or her. Imagine that you're standing at the edge of a huge cliff, with your back to the cliff. At the bottom are numerous jagged rocks that will cut you to pieces if you fall. Realize that your life is on the line; everything you have, everything you will ever have is at stake. If you take one wrong step, it will be all over; you will plunge to your death.

STEP 2. Fall backward, and have your mate catch you. If you're much bigger than your partner, ask him or her to lean against a wall for support (or have a friend back your partner up) as you fall.

You may need to do this several times before you feel completely comfortable letting yourself fall back with your entire body weight. In the beginning you may let yourself fall back only a little bit because you're not sure you can trust your partner to catch you.

STEP 3. Repeat Step 2, except this time your partner will fall, and you will catch him or her.

STEP 4. Discuss this exercise with your partner. Mention that falling backward is like giving your love and life to your partner. The exercise is symbolic of the level of trust, commitment, and faith that two people must bring to a relationship if it is to be intimate, loving, and long-lasting.

Trust is not a one-time thing; it's a process. Continue to do this exercise until both of you are able to fall back and land in each other's arms without any hesitation whatsoever. Keep practicing until you and your partner are secure in the knowledge that you can trust each other completely, without reservation.

By doing this exercise from the very beginning of your relationship, you will build a marvelous sense of trust in each other. You will go a long way toward cementing the bonds of love and connection that will turn your relationship into a successful joint venture.

The Sex Observer:
The Impostor at the Door

The intruders silently crept into the bedroom, where Luke and Denise lay naked, fondling and caressing each other. It was the moment of truth for the young lovers; they had been dating for six months and cared deeply for each other. Now they were ready to take their relationship to the next level and make love for the first time. As they kissed and played with each other, they were too distracted to notice the intruders as they crept in.

Dangerous and cat-quick, the intruders, aka the Sex Observers, methodically picked their targets and unleashed their devastating assaults on their unsuspecting prey: "You're going to come too quickly like always," sneered the Sex Observer who had sneaked into Luke's head. "It's been so long since you've been with a woman, you probably forgot where to put it." Meanwhile, Denise's Sex Observer had broken in: "You don't know how to please a man. You're so inexperienced; he'll be really disappointed in you. And don't you dare moan. If you let loose like you want to, he'll think you're a slut."

As the Sex Observers did their dirty work, Luke and Denise thought twice about what they were about to do.

"Maybe we shouldn't rush this," said Denise, afraid she wouldn't be experienced enough to please Luke.

"OK, I guess," replied Luke, certain that Denise knew how sexually incompetent he was. Why else would she back out now?

Yes, the Observer has an evil twin, the Sex Observer, whose sole aim is to plant doubts in your mind and make you feel inadequate whenever you think about making love with your partner: Will he (or she) find me attractive? How hard/soft/fast/slow should I touch her? Will I be able to please him? Will I get an erection/orgasm big enough to satisfy my lover? Although some of these questions are legitimate and important, you can bet the Sex Observer is already stuffing all the wrong answers into your head to make you feel like a complete loser in the bedroom.

Yet no matter how many times the Sex Observer has tormented you in the past, it's your turn to do to the Sex Observer what you did to the original Observer in Chapter 5: Put it away in the basement, where it belongs.

Exercise 4. Kick the Sex Observer out of Your Sex Life

Here's an effective exercise to help you mute the Sex Observer and keep it out of your bedroom.

STEP 1. With your eyes closed, think back to a time when you thought about making love to someone special and all those negative and self-conscious Sex Observer thoughts popped up. Visualize what the Sex Observer looked like in your head as it wreaked havoc on your love life.

STEP 2. Cut out a picture from a book, magazine, or newspaper that reminds you of the Sex Observer. If you like to draw, get some crayons, markers, or colored pencils and draw the Sex Observer exactly as you envision it. Include all the ugly details you can think of—all the warts, moles, and scars on its nasty face.

STEP 3. Take out your drawing or photo, and study the Sex Observer's face carefully. From Step 1, review all the self-critical thoughts it tried to implant in your mind when you wanted to make love with a desirable person.

Now think of all the terrific sexual experiences you could have enjoyed if only the Sex Observer had not interfered and spoiled everything. Remember that special person you were dying to make love to and how the Sex Observer pulled you back at the last minute. Recall that special moment when you wanted to try something fun and experimental in bed and the Sex Observer grabbed you by the genitals and made you feel like a fool for even considering it.

STEP 4. Stand up, and with as much force as possible, tell the Sex Observer exactly what you think of it. Let yourself go: Scream, rant, and rave; stomp your feet, jump up and down, roll on the floor. Do whatever it takes to let the truth out: You're sick and tired of the Sex Observer, and you don't want it in your sex life anymore!

You might say something like: "You impotent knucklehead, Sex Observer! I want you out of my sex life forever. I'm a sexy, vital, playful, and loving person who deserves to be in a sexually satisfying and rewarding relationship with my soul mate. I don't need you in my life. Get out, Sex Observer!"

STEP 5. The next time you're in a sexually intimate situation and the Sex Observer rears its ugly head, repeat Step 4: Tell the Sex Observer to get out of your life.

Although the Sex Observer is generally a destructive force, it does have one useful function: It can serve as your sexual conscience and protector so you don't do something foolish and unhealthy. The Sex Observer can, for example, remind you to put your condom on, to take your birth control pills. It can warn you to be certain someone is safe and trustworthy before you sleep with him or her.

Just like the original Observer, the Sex Observer belongs in that 20 to 30 percent of your mind where it will come in handy to protect you from harm. By listening to the Sex Observer about 20 to 30 percent of the time, you can protect yourself from bad sexual experiences, sexually transmitted diseases, and unwanted pregnancies. These are all important things to think about, and the Sex Observer will do all this thinking for you. But you still need to know when to draw the line. When the Sex Observer intrudes on your love life and tries to make you feel ashamed, anxious, and inadequate, it's time to lock the Sex Observer in the closet until it's ready to behave.

Awakening Your Sex Actor

While you're working to bring your Sex Observer under control, you should also be developing your Sex Actor—the part of you that is secure, confident, and spontaneous when it comes to sex. Whereas the Sex Observer encourages you to regard sex as shameful and embarrassing, the Sex Actor wants you to realize that you're a sexual being who has legitimate needs and wants, and that you have the right to fulfill those desires in a responsible and loving way. When your Sex Actor is in charge, you will recognize that making love with the right partner can be playful, fun, mysterious, exciting, pleasurable, and sacred.

The Sex Actor in you is not only fun-loving and spontaneous but also aware, intelligent, and patient. It has an impeccable sense of timing and is able to recognize the ideal moment to approach someone sexually. Rather than rush into a romantic situation unprepared (the way the Sex Observer urges you to do) and ruin the moment, the Sex Actor tells you to take your time and make sure the moment and person are right.

When you start spending time with someone, the Sex Actor tells you to wait until you're fully in sync with that individual before you make or accept any sexual overtures. It recommends that you spend quite of bit a time with this person, communicating as deeply and intimately as possible before you take things to a sexual level. Because you have a shy-sensitive nature, sex can be an intimidating experience for you. Let the Sex Actor guide you slowly and comfortably through the process.

How do you develop this sexy Actor? By working on yourself from the inside out. Although it's important to take care of your physical appearance through proper diet, exercise, grooming, and dress, your sexiness needs to originate from inside your mind.

Begin by watching people in the real world (or characters from TV and movies) who have a strong aura of sexiness. Notice how they dress, walk, talk, and carry themselves. They may not be the most physically beautiful people in the world, but there's usually something special about them that attracts people to them like crazy. Study these individuals, and pick your favorite role models.

Practice their mannerisms, behaviors, and speaking styles in front of a mirror; try on some of the clothes they like to wear. Determine which of their traits, attitudes, and preferences you would like to incorporate into your own Sex Actor.

No, you don't need to be just like them; you will still keep your unique shy-sensitive style. You may find that some of the things your sexy role model does and says feel comfortable and natural for you while others don't. Just adopt those behaviors and attitudes that work for you and discard the rest. Once you start to feel the Sex Actor growing inside you and boosting your self-confidence, it's time to incorporate this wonderful friend into your love life.

One caveat: Go slowly. Gradually work yourself up to trying new things in bed. Don't do everything all at once.

As you begin to develop your Sex Actor, you will find yourself becoming more spontaneous and confident when making love. There will be times, however, when you will still feel uncomfortable about fully expressing your sexual desires. Your self-consciousness will pull you back. When that happens, don't worry about it; developing your Sex Actor takes time and patience. If you allow your Sex Actor to come out a little bit more each time, you will soon be able to enjoy a fun, spontaneous, and creative sex life without shame or guilt.

Exercise 5. Your Sex Actor Is in Your Bedroom

In this exercise each step represents a level of the Sex Actor, from the most basic to the most advanced. Before you begin take some time to think about your present comfort level and where you want to start. You may decide that you would be comfortable doing only Step 1. Or you may feel you're ready to try all three.

STEP 1. Make up a sexy story or scene, and write it down. Perhaps you will write about a primitive island girl who is rescued by a handsome sea captain and makes love with him aboard his mighty ship. Once you're satisfied with your story, read it aloud to yourself. To get your partner into the act, tuck the sexy story in an envelope and leave it for your lover in a private place where he or she will find it. Add a dab of lipstick and perfume (or cologne) to the envelope for a nice sexy touch. You can also E-mail the story to your partner (but make sure no one else reads his or her E-mails).

STEP 2. Incorporate erotic words and sounds into your lovemaking to heighten your pleasure. If you can't bring yourself to say erotic words at first, begin with moans and sounds like *Ooooohh, ahhhh,* and so forth.

Another option: Describe what your partner is doing to you (and what you're doing to your partner) as you make love: "You're touching my face gently. I'm licking your nipples with my wet tongue." Even if you say these words in a neutral, run-of-the-mill manner, you and your partner are bound to get aroused because you're tapping into powerful word pictures.

STEP 3. Use role playing to put your Sex Actor into play. Start with a straightforward question and answer session with your mate, asking about the characters you will play:

- What is this person wearing?
- What is his or her body like?
- How does this person speak?
- What kind of personality does he or she have?
- What is this person's profession?
- What does this person want from me?

Once you've decided on the details, one of you will excuse yourself, then make a grand entrance as that character, while the other partner responds as the character he or she has selected. (For more tips on how to play different roles as the Actor, review Part 2.)

If you want to get really creative, try incorporating your shy persona into your role playing. For example, if you're the shy one, you can play a shy virgin football player while your partner plays an aggressive cheerleader who teaches you how to score a real touchdown. Whatever you do, make sure you have fun, and let your Sex Actor come out and play, a little bit more each time, until there's nothing but steamy passion and romance in your sex life.

Who wants to get out of bed now?

Relationship Combinations

Although they were deeply in love and had a satisfying relationship after four years together, Tony, a forty-five-year-old sales manager, and Audrey, a forty-three-year-old actuary, didn't always see eye to eye. As a shy person, Audrey felt especially anxious in social settings where she feared people might judge her. Tony, by contrast, wasn't shy, and he loved hanging out with his large circle of friends. He wanted to include Audrey in these good times because he believed it would bring them closer.

Fat chance, thought Audrey. The last thing she wanted was to share Tony with a bunch of people she barely knew. She wanted to spend quiet evenings with him at home, watching movies, cuddling, talking, and making love by the fireplace. Sure, an occasional night out was OK, but not on a regular basis.

Fortunately, Tony and Audrey went to couples counseling and were able to work out their differences after learning more about each other's styles. To please Audrey, Tony agreed to spend plenty of solo time with her—taking quiet walks along the beach, enjoying fine dining at intimate restaurants, and watching classic movies. To please Tony, Audrey would occasionally join him and his friends—the ones who were more sensitive and gentle—and she would give him a boys' night out once in a while.

Now that they accept and understand each other, their fights have been greatly reduced. They enjoy each other's company without trying to change each other, and they use their differences as assets to enhance their relationship and keep it growing, day by day.

OK, so now you trust your partner, you're enjoying a great sex life, and everything is perfect, right? Well, maybe not 100 percent perfect. Even if your relationship is a supremely compatible one, you will probably have some conflicts once in a while. That's just part of life. The key is to work out any differences before they become major arguments and fights.

In this section we will take a brief look at some of the challenges you and your partner may face, depending on your shy type combination. If you learn about these issues now—before they damage your relationship—you can take the right steps to defuse potentially serious conflicts and develop a more harmonious and loving relationship.

When You and Your Partner Are Shy

When both of you are shy, you can have a harmonious relationship because you understand each other so well and share so many social interests and goals. When you spend time together, it's like being in a cozy, safe haven where you can relax from the stresses of life. As you shut yourselves off from the rest of the world, you and your partner can happily explore each other's bodies, minds, and souls. As empathetic lovers, you and your partner can serve as each other's counselors and healers—listening deeply to each other's feelings and caring for each other's needs.

Now that you know some of the benefits of being with a shy person like yourself, let's take a look at some of the challenges you may face and how you can handle them.

Challenge 1. Hiding the Conflict

Because both of you hate conflict, you may hide resentments and postpone arguments until the problems build up and explode into loud and nasty fights that can do some serious damage to your relationship.

FIXING THE TROUBLE. Sit down with your partner and discuss how you will handle any conflicts that come up. Agree that you will seek a middle ground—neither ignoring conflicts until they become big fights nor engaging in constant, energy-draining petty arguments.

Set limits to your arguments: Agree that you will keep discussing an issue as long as neither of you is feeling too angry or overwhelmed. If you or your partner starts feeling upset or pressured, you will use techniques such as time out (interrupting the discussion and leaving the room to cool off), meditation, and deep breathing to deescalate the situation and bring harmony and peace back into the discussion.

Challenge 2. Doing Too Much for Your Mate: The Martyr Complex

Because both of you are very sensitive to each other's needs, you and your partner may exhaust yourselves trying to please each other, then feel guilty because you didn't do more.

FIXING THE TROUBLE. Both of you need to step back and realize that there is an important distinction between being generous and being a martyr. Being generous to your mate means that you offer affection and support in a mature and intelligent way, whereas being a martyr means you hold the unrealistic idea that you must sacrifice yourself, and even experience pain, to prove your love.

You and your partner need to recognize that neither of you has to suffer for the other. In a healthy relationship, both partners can give to each other wholeheartedly while still holding something back to take care of their own needs. In fact, taking care of your own needs is one of the most loving things you can do for your partner. When you're relaxed and contented, your partner will be able to share in your good feelings.

Discuss this issue with your partner, and agree that from now on you will seek a middle ground: Both of you will give to each other from the bottom of your hearts while also respecting each other's personal needs for rest and self-care.

Challenge 3. When Cozy Becomes Boring

Because you and your partner see the relationship as a safe haven, there's a danger that boredom may creep in. You may end up falling into a repetitive cycle—watching videos, lying around the house—that can cut the novelty and excitement right out of your relationship. When this happens you and your partner may stop looking for excitement within the relationship and start searching for it elsewhere—thereby opening up the possibility of jealousies, affairs, and, ultimately, a shattered relationship.

FIXING THE TROUBLE. You should always put your relationship first. Instead of reserving your best energy for outside social activities, save it for each other. Schedule some fun and exciting activities that you can enjoy with your partner: Explore new places, read to each other, make love in different locations and ways, learn a new hobby together, or take an exotic trip.

When You're Shy and
Your Partner Isn't

As social opposites, you and your non-shy partner can balance and complement each other nicely as long as you respect each other's styles. When you're shy and your mate isn't, you can relax and lay back in social situations. You can let your non-shy partner do the social work—networking, mingling, and introducing you to new people—while you kick back in your shy cocoon until you're ready to make an appearance. From your partner's point of view, you bring sensitivity, relaxation, and a nice comfort level to the relationship. Your partner will appreciate your peaceful and sensitive style and the way you calm him or her down after a frenzy of social activity.

That's the good stuff; now here are some difficulties you may en-counter and how to deal with them.

Challenge 1. Dealing with the Warm-Up Period

As a shy person, you need a considerable warm-up period for many things in life, especially when you're interacting with people. If your non-shy partner doesn't understand your need for a warm-up period, he or she will probably become impatient with what ap-pear to be your dragging feet and indecisive mind-set. From your non-shy partner's perspective, it would be much better if you would move into social situations more quickly, make decisions faster, and get things out in the open sooner. When your partner pressures you like this, you will feel resentful and angry.

FIXING THE TROUBLE. Each of you needs to respect each other's style. First of all, you need to recognize that your non-shy partner is not trying to be mean or pushy; he or she just wants to get things moving and make progress in the relationship. Your partner believes that the longer you delay going to a planned social event, or the more time you take making a simple decision, the more you'll put a damper on the relationship and prevent the two of you from having an enjoyable life together.

Although you may not fully agree with your partner's approach, give him or her the benefit of the doubt. Try to get ready a little more quickly for social events; make up your mind about things a bit faster. Don't compromise your deeply held values, but try to give your partner a tad more of that "go get 'em" mentality he or she favors.

At the same time, your partner needs to recognize how important it is for you to warm up to situations. Because of your sensitive nature, you need extra time to get used to new environments. Moreover, with your deep, reflective mind, you can see more possibilities, and you need more time to consider them all before you come up with a definite conclusion. If your partner can give you the extra time you need to warm up socially, and the additional time you require to make decisions, he or she will find that you will be a much happier and more accommodating mate, and you will be more than willing to take care of your partner's needs as well.

Challenge 2. Dealing with Social Sensitivity

If you're shy, you may feel anxious when you go to social events, especially if important and high-status people are present. When your partner sees how ultrasensitive you are in these situations, he or she may wish you could be like a normal person who isn't so freaked out by other people's reactions. And you may resent the fact that your partner can be so insensitive at times. When you least expect it, your partner is likely to say something that makes you feel like crawling under the carpet. You hate it when your partner does that, but he or she just keeps doing it.

FIXING THE TROUBLE. Both of you need to understand each other's approach to social interactions. You need to realize that your non-shy partner is not really being insensitive or trying to embarrass you in social settings; your mate is just being direct and straightforward about things. Because your partner is not as worried as you are about how other people will react, he or she feels free to speak directly and candidly. Your non-shy partner needs to understand that your feelings can be hurt, and you can be easily embarrassed in social settings. Your partner needs to be more careful with what he or she says when you're present. In fact, your partner would be wise to ask himself or herself these questions before speaking up: How will my speech and actions affect my mate? Will I embarrass my partner? Will I make my partner feel more comfortable or less?

Challenge 3. Dealing with Personal Space

As a shy person, you probably need a significant amount of private space and downtime apart from your mate so you can relax and take care of yourself. Your non-shy partner may not need as much private space and personal time, and he or she may accuse you of being distant and cold. Your partner will then try to pressure you into spending more time with him or her even when you're not ready to do so. When your partner is pushy like that, you're likely to feel resentful, and you may wonder if your mate really understands your needs.

FIXING THE TROUBLE. Again, the key is for both of you to understand, and accept, each other's differences. First of all, you need to see your partner's request for more time together as proof that he or she loves you. When you see it this way, you may decide to compromise a little and share more of yourself. At the same time, your partner needs to understand how important your personal space and time are to you. Because you have such a sensitive nature, you need a significant amount of private and quiet time to recuperate from the harshness and insensitivity of the outside world.

Your non-shy partner can make life easier for you by giving you the space and time you need to unwind and relax. For example, when you come home after a long, hard day at work, your non-shy partner can encourage you to spend some time alone—reading, writing, thinking, and meditating—until you're ready to spend quality time with him or her.

By understanding and respecting each other's differences in this way, you can make great strides in improving your relationship and creating a successful partnership that lasts.

It's Your Shy World Now:
Live It, Be It, Love It

We've made it to the end of your movie now: The last scene is up on the screen, the theme song is playing, and the lights are ready to come on. For the past few hours, you've been watching the movie of your shy romantic life on the screen of your imagination, filling your mind with images from your past, present, and ultimately your future.

It all started with you, the star of the show, and your desire to connect with your soul mate, the leading man or lady in your life. Early on, you got a break when you discovered hidden treasure—the Gift of Shyness—right there under your own skin. For years this treasure had lain unclaimed and ignored by the so-called treasure experts until you discovered the well-documented treasure map. Once you dug up your Gift of Shyness, you had all the resources you needed to find your soul mate.

Helping you along the way was the Actor, your spontaneous, fun-loving sidekick who taught you how to take chances—and get your fools out—so you could finally be free to meet the person of your dreams. Working against you was the Observer, that nasty little villain who did everything in its power to make you doubt your romantic worthiness. Although the Observer had its moments, it was no match for your superhero Actor. In the end the Observer was nothing more than a puny distraction, a tiny speed bump, on your way to unqualified romantic success.

As you reached the pinnacle of romantic triumph and came within moments of meeting your ideal mate, you came to an amazing realization:

THE GENIE INSIDE THE MAGIC BOTTLE WAS YOU ALL ALONG: YOU WERE THE ONLY THING YOU EVER NEEDED TO MAKE YOUR ROMANTIC DREAMS COME TRUE.

That's right; it wasn't family and friends, matchmakers, dating services, tapes, books, or anything else that put you in the perfect position to meet the right person. It was your shy-sensitive nature that held the key.

All you had to do was embrace this nature fully, and the rest was easy. It was simply a matter of applying your new skills and insights to the dating world, and before you knew it you were ready to meet the love of your life.

It's time now. The movie is ending; the final scene is playing. It's you, at the airport, waiting to board the last plane of the evening—the one that will take you to the person of your dreams. You have your ticket, your bags are stored onboard, and you're on your way to love—carrying with you your most valuable possession: the Gift of Shyness.

Notes

CHAPTER 2. IT'S A SHY WORLD AFTER ALL

p. 19   "At least 40 percent of Americans" B. Carducci and P. Zimbardo, "Are You Shy?" *Psychology Today* Nov.–Dec. 1995.

p. 21   "many U.S. mothers tend to feel concerned" X. Chen, K. Rubin, G. Cen, P. Hastings, H. Chen, and S. Stewart, "Child-Rearing Attitudes and Behavioral Inhibition in Chinese and Canadian Toddlers: A Cross-Cultural Study," *Developmental Psychology* 34 (1998).

p. 23   "Emotional reactivity appears to have a genetic base" J. Kagan, "Temperament and the Reactions to Unfamiliarity," *Child Development* 68 (1997).

p. 26   "the more men think about women" E. M. Mahone, M. Bruch, and R. Heimberg, "Focus of Attention and Social Anxiety: The Role of Negative Self-Thoughts and Perceived Positive Attributes of the Other," *Cognitive Therapy and Research* 17 (1993).

p. 28   "In support of this theory" J. Kagan, J. S. Reznick, and N. Snidman, "The Physiology and Psychology of Behavioral Inhibition in Children," *Child Development* 58 (1987).

p. 30   "Back in 1985 researchers found" C. R. Snyder, T. Smith, R. W. Augelli, and R. E. Ingram, "On the Self-Serving Function of Social Anxiety: Shyness as a Self-Handicapping Strategy," *Journal of Personality and Social Psychology* 48 (1985).

p. 30   "Only six years later, however, another study found" J. R. McNamara and K. Grossman, "Initiation of Dates and Anxiety Among College Men and Women," *Psychological Reports* 69 (1991).

p. 30   "men, when selecting their prospective mates" D. Buss and D. Schmitt, "Sexual Strategies Theory: An Evolutionary Perspective on Human Mating," *Psychological Review* 100 (1993).

p. 31   "two-thirds of the American women observed" T. Perper, *Sex Signals: The Biology of Love* (Philadelphia: ISI Press, 1985). See also D. B. Givens, *How to Attract a Mate* (New York: Crown, 1983).

p. 33   "In Shanghai, China, children who are shy" X. Chen, K. Rubin, and Y. Sun, "Social Reputation and Peer Relationships in Chinese and Canadian Children: A Cross-Cultural Study," *Child Development* 63 (1992).

CHAPTER 3. THE SEVEN GIFTS OF SHYNESS

p. 41   "in a study with second- and fourth-grade Chinese children" X. Chen, K. Rubin, B. Li, and D. Li, "Adolescent Outcomes of Social Functioning in Chinese Children," *International Journal of Behavioral Development* 23 (1999).

p. 44   "shy people . . . tend to be more monogamous" M. Parks, K. Dindia, J. Adams, E. Berlin, and K. Larson, "Communication Apprehension and Student Dating Patterns: A Replication and Extension," *Communication Quarterly* 28 (Spring 1981).

p. 44   "the spouses and long-term partners of shy people" H. G. Gough and A. Thorne, "Positive, Negative, and Balanced Shyness: Self-Definitions and the Reactions of Others," in *Shyness: Perspectives on Research and Treatment*, edited by W. Jones, J. Cheek, and S. Briggs (New York: Plenum Press, 1986).

p. 47   "In a study of vocal activity and listening ability" J. Daly, J. C. McCroskey, and V. P. Richmond, "Judgements of Quality, Listening, and Understanding Based upon Vocal Quality," *Southern Speech Communication Journal* 41 (Winter 1976).

p. 47   "shy people are sensitive listeners" A. Clark, "Communication Confidence and Listening Competence: An Investigation of the Relationships of Willingness to Communicate, Communication Apprehension, and Receiver Apprehension to Comprehension of Content and Emotional Meaning in Spoken Messages," *Communication Education* 38 (1989).

p. 58   "shy people go out of their way to please" M. Leary, P. Knight, and K. Johnson, "Social Anxiety and Dyadic Conversation: A Verbal Response Analysis," *Journal of Social and Clinical Psychology* 5 (1987).

p. 69 "Until recently Introverts were the minority" C. R. Martin, "Estimated Frequencies of the Types in the United States Population" (Gainesville, Fla.: Center for Applications of Psychological Type, 1996).

CHAPTER 4. WHAT KIND OF SHY AM I?

p. 71 "Researchers have compared the two factors" A. Buss, "A Dual Conception of Shyness," in *Avoiding Communication: Shyness, Reticence, and Communication Apprehension* 2nd ed. (Cresskill, N.J.: Hampton Press, 1997).

CHAPTER 5. BATTLING FOR YOUR ROMANTIC LIFE

p. 82 "shy men tend to view their dating failures" A. Avila, "Understanding the Attributions of Shy Versus Non-Shy Males in First Encounters with the Opposite Sex" (Ph.D. diss., California School of Professional Psychology, 1998).

p. 95 "socially successful people have approximately 70 to 80 percent" S. Zelen, "Balance and Reversal of Actor-Observer Perspectives: An Attributional Model of Pathology," *Journal of Social and Clinical Psychology* 5 (1987).

CHAPTER 8. COMMUNICATING WITH YOUR ENTIRE ESSENCE

p. 128 "researchers investigated the differences between Japanese and American attitudes" M. Wayne, "An Experimental Study in the Meaning of Silence in Three Cultures" (M.A. thesis, International Christian University, 1973).

p. 138 "According to proxemics" E. T. Hall, *The Hidden Dimension* (New York: Doubleday, 1966).

p. 139 "shy people prefer to keep more space" B. Carducci and A. Webber, "Shyness as a Determinant of Interpersonal Distance," *Psychological Reports* 44 (1979).

CHAPTER 10. HOW TO BE A SHY TYPE DETECTIVE

p. 173 "the problems Introvert men tend to have" R. Sherman, "Typology and Problems in Intimate Relationships," *Research in Psychological Type* 4 (1981).

Suggested Readings
and Websites

SUGGESTED READINGS

Aron, Elaine. *The Highly Sensitive Person: How to Thrive When the World Overwhelms You*. Secaucus, N.J.: Carol Publishing Group, 1996.

Avila, Alexander. *LoveTypes: Discover Your Romantic Style and Find Your Soul Mate*. New York: Avon Books, 1999.

Botting, Kate, and Douglas Botting. *Sex Appeal: The Art and Science of Sexual Attraction*. New York: St. Martin's Press, 1993.

Campbell, Joseph, ed. *The Portable Jung*. New York: Viking Penguin, 1971. (Pay special attention to Chapter 8 on the psychological types.)

De Angelis, Barbara. *Are You the One for Me?* New York: Dell, 1992.

Fast, Julius. *Body Language*. New York: Pocket Books, 1970.

Girodo, Michel. *Shy? You Don't Have to Be*. New York: Pocket Books, 1978.

Hall, Edward T. *The Hidden Dimension*. New York: Doubleday, 1966.

Johnstone, Keith. *Impro: Improvisation and the Theatre*. New York: Theatre Arts Books, 1979.

Jones, Phil. *Drama as Therapy: Theatre as Living*. New York: Routledge, 1996.

Karp, Marcia, Paul Holmes, and Kate Tauvon, eds. *The Handbook of Psychodrama*. New York: Routledge, 1998.

Keller, Betty. *Improvisations in Creative Drama*. Colorado Springs, Colo.: Meriwether, 1988.

Lloyd-Elliot, Martin. *Secrets of Sexual Body Language*. Berkeley, Calif.: Ulysses Press, 1996.

Schneier, Franklin, and Lawrence Welkowitz. *The Hidden Face of Shyness.* New York: Avon Books, 1996.

Wolf, Sharyn. *Fifty Ways to Find a Lover: Proven Techniques for Finding Someone Special.* Holbrook, Mass.: Adams Media, 1992.

WEBSITES

www.giftofshyness.com: This is our official website with cutting-edge information, research, products, and services to help shy people maximize their dating success and achieve their romantic dreams.

www.shyandfree.com: This is an excellent shy-positive website with a lot of interesting information about shyness, as well as links to other shyness sites.

Shyness Research Questionnaire Free Bonus Gift: Special Report

Dear Reader:

In the interest of ongoing shyness research, we would be grateful if you would fill out and return the following short questionnaire. As a bonus gift for filling it out, we will send you—*free—Special Report 1: How to Be Shy and Irresistible.*

We will keep your answers confidential and use them only for the documentation of our shyness research.

Also, we would love to hear your success stories. Tell us how you used the Gift of Shyness system to transform your shyness and achieve your romantic dreams. Please return this form to the address on page 239.

Fill in and circle the answer(s) that apply to you:

Name: _____

Gender: _____

Shy Type (from Chapter 4): _____

Race/Ethnicity: Caucasian   Hispanic

Asian   African American

Native American   Other _____

Educational Status: Some High School

High School Graduate

Some College

College Graduate

Some Graduate School

Graduate Degree (M.B.A., M.A., Ph.D., J.D.)

Occupation: _____

Age: _____

Address: _____

Phone: _____

E-mail: _____

Relationship Status: Married   Separated

Divorced   Never Married

Widowed

In the past, your most compatible relationship was with someone who was most likely (circle the social styles he or she primarily exhibited):

Introvert   Extravert   Shy   Non-shy

Comments _____

_____

Thank you very much.

Please send this questionnaire to: The Gift of Shyness
P.O. Box 40
Alhambra, CA 91802

· or E-mail answers to
giftofshyness@aol.com

Free Gift of
Shyness Dating
Success Catalog

You can start enjoying dating success today by requesting your *free* Gift of Shyness Dating Success Catalog and using the following cutting-edge ImprovTherapy innovations:

Personal Shyness Coaching: Consult with the shy dating expert, Dr. Alexander Avila, as he helps you design a customized romantic plan that accentuates your gift of shyness and minimizes your weaknesses, en route to helping you fulfill your romantic dreams. You can receive shy dating mastery coaching by E-mail, on-line chatting, phone, or in person when Dr. Avila travels on one of his many worldwide trips. Call now for your *free* initial consultation.

ImprovTherapy Groups: Get involved in a fun and empowering ImprovTherapy group near you. Develop your social Actor skills in a fun, safe, and comfortable setting. Meet like-minded shy and Introverted people and make new friends, on your way to becoming the master of your social and romantic universe.

Gift of Shyness Cassettes and Videos: Learn cutting-edge strategies and field-proven techniques for transforming your shyness into a dating advantage that irresistibly attracts the person of your dreams.

Gift of Shyness Special Reports: These special reports contain the latest shyness research and offer invaluable strategies for embracing your shy side, developing more of your Actor, minimizing your Observer, and creating successful relationships that last a lifetime. Topics range from *How to Love a Non-Shy Partner* to *How to Be Shy and Irresistible*.

- **Gift of Shyness Newsletter:** Subscribe to the only newsletter that lists available singles by their shy type, and place as many free personal ads as you want. Expand your social network and meet your ideal match as you read about cutting edge shyness research developments, dating tactics, and success stories.

To learn more about these offers or to receive your *free* Gift of Shyness Catalog contact me personally at:

The Gift of Shyness

P.O. Box 40

Alhambra, CA 91802

Toll-Free Phone: 1-888-568-8973

E-mail: giftofshyness@aol.com

Website: www.giftofshyness.com

Index